REMARRIAGE

Larry Richards

REMARRIAGE

A Healing Gift From God

WORD PUBLISHING
Dallas·London·Vancouver·Melbourne

for Joan and her friends

Contents

A Personal Word

When I was asked to study remarriage by the dear friend to whom this book is dedicated, I did so with hesitation. Before graduating from seminary I had explored the area and traced all the arguments of commentators. I felt that I had come to a biblical position: that remarriage is an option only for those whose ex-spouses have previously remarried. But recently I have become acquainted with the many hurts in the Christian community caused by the breakup of marriages. I have talked with ministers in churches where remarried believers number as high as 40 percent of the congregation. All these ministers are deeply concerned, but unable to deal confidently with the situations they confront. The Bible's teachings simply seem too complex to demand a legalistic "never!" But at the same time the ministers are concerned about remaining true to the Word and will of God.

So I began to pray about this area and earnestly seek to know God's heart as well as mind. While speaking

Remarriage

at a Sunday school convention in Wichita, Kansas, I
had a number of free hours in my room. At that time
I began the study I had promised Joan to do. I firmly
expected that the conclusions I reached would be the
same I had drawn when I did this study some years
ago in Dallas.

I approached the passages in what I found to be
the only sound method of biblical interpretation: tracing the argument of the total passage in which the
focal statements are found. I was stunned. Each new
passage seemed to suggest more and more surprising
insights.

The key insight from Matthew 19 is that Jesus, in
dealing with the Pharisees, is demonstrating that Law
does not express an ideal but grace. Law reveals God's
willingness to accommodate himself to our hardness
of heart. I had developed this concept earlier when
writing *The Servant King*, a study of the life of Christ
published by David C. Cook Publishing Company as
part of the *Bible Alive* study series. But the implications of this teaching, focused fully on marriage, led
me to a position which goes beyond the "forgivable
sin" concept presented in Andre Bustanoby's excellent
book, *But I Don't Want a Divorce.* As I compared
each Gospel and 1 Corinthians 7, seeing that Paul and
Jesus both use exceptionless form statements which
do have exceptions, and thus specifically validate remarriage, I came to believe that remarriage is a valid
option for Christians.

At this point I considered whether I should share
this view with my friend Joan only, or make it available
to the Christian community. The more I reviewed the
concepts, and thought of people I know who are trapped in tragic "hardness of heart" situations, I felt I
must risk sharing with the Body at large.

I am aware that this is, to say the least, a controversial
book. My other ministries may be adversely affected.

I certainly expect attack and misunderstanding. But the thought of the thousands and thousands who are suffering, and who need our compassion rather than our condemnation, and my personal conviction that the teaching in this book is in harmony with both the letter and the spirit of Christ's good Word left me no alternative.

And so I present this book to you. My appeal is a simple one. Do not reject what this book suggests without studying the Scriptures, and without much prayer. If you do reject it, at least extend to me, and to others who may agree with it, the right to be responsible to Jesus Christ, who is Lord and who is the sole Judge of the thoughts and motives of our hearts. And, please, treat the suffering brothers and sisters among us with the one thing which Jesus always showed to those to whom he ministered.

Mercy.

And compassion.

LARRY RICHARDS

to be read with compassion

PART I

The Problems

1

Doorway

Diana hadn't been prepared. She'd never expected this! Di pushed Frank away, but she was shaken. Shaken by the surge of feelings that were far more than sexual. Feelings that revealed the great need just to be held and comforted, to share herself with someone, that she had denied and pushed away during the agonizing months leading up to the divorce.

Diana, as a new Christian, hadn't wanted a divorce. At thirty-two, with two small children, she had desperately wanted her marriage to work. But Hank had very different ideas. He had only wanted a live-in housekeeper and lover. And his freedom. She'd known Hank was immature when they were married eight years before. But she hadn't expected the selfishness, the total disregard for her as a person, that set the pattern of their married life. Hank was a good provider. He made plenty of money, and they never went without any material comfort. But each weekend, and often for weeks at a time, Hank would just leave. He roamed with his friends, skied, partied in Las Vegas, and God only knew what else. When Diana pled with him, he became cold and angry and physically abusive.

Diana didn't know when she'd started thinking about divorce. Probably after she'd begun to share her problems with the small Bible study group that met at Carol's house. There she found warmth and under-standing and real caring. The other women prayed for her, and for the first time in her life, Diana too began to talk to God as though he might be alive. In time Diana accepted Jesus Christ as her personal Savior and found a sense of release and belonging she'd never known.

Hank had been angry about her turning to religion. But Hank seemed to get angry about everything she did. Diana knew that the abusive pattern was deepen-ing. Now even in their most intimate times Hank seemed to delight in hurting her.

Finally Diana felt she couldn't stand it any longer. She filed for divorce. Diana didn't want to divorce Hank. She felt divorce was wrong. And she honestly wanted to please God. But Diana was becoming more and more afraid of her husband. What if he really did hurt her one day? What would the children do? Certainly Hank never seemed to care about them. Without her they'd be left alone!

The time of waiting for the divorce was an agonizing one. Diana alternately felt a sense of exhilarating free-dom and then guilt. The thought of not having to wait in fear for Hank's next return or next desertion brought such relief. But the certainty that divorce was wrong, and the terrible doubt about God's attitude toward her as a divorcee, often weighed her down with an anguished sense of guilt and shame.

It was several months after the divorce came that she and a girl friend had gone to the country club for dinner. The dance music from the hall next door drew them in after the meal. For a time they sat and watched. Then someone asked Di's friend to dance. And soon Di found herself on the dance floor too; caught up in the music, having *fun* for the first time in years!

That night Diana danced and laughed and felt again the sense of confidence that came from knowing she was healthy and attractive and desirable as a woman.

But then Frank had walked her to the car. Suddenly his arms slipped around her, and he actually lifted her up off the ground, cradling her, and began to carry her toward *his* car. Frightened, she cried out and pushed away. But she was more frightened of herself than of him.

Later, sharing the experience, Diana talked about what she had discovered in that moment. "I didn't know I was so vulnerable," she said. "When I divorced Hank, I was determined never to remarry. As a Christian, I felt that divorce is wrong, but that God would understand why I had to do it. I've been told that remarriage, though, is something God can't forgive. So I committed myself to put all that behind me.

"But when Frank held me . . . well . . . I realized how much I need to be loved. And how vulnerable I am to being loved. If the right man came along, and proposed, I . . . I don't know if I could live up to my commitment. No, I know I couldn't.

"I'm only thirty-two. What am I going to do?"

Today there are hundreds of thousands of men and women caught in Diana's dilemma. They have been through a divorce, or are going through that painful process now. They may know that more than 80 percent of those who divorce will remarry, but many are uncertain about remarriage. Doesn't the Bible teach that remarriage is adultery?

Those who are Christians (and there are many Christians today who know the pain of divorce) have lived

Remarriage

under specific teaching against divorce and remarriage. In the Christian community today divorce is gaining greater acceptance, and those who have known divorce may sense more support than judgment. But there are still deep-seated convictions against remarriage. "A wife must not separate from her husband," the New Testament teaches. "But if she does, she must remain unmarried or else be reconciled to her husband. And a husband must not divorce his wife" (1 Cor. 7:10–11). This clear statement seems to indicate that while divorce is wrong, under some circumstances it may happen. But when it does happen, there is never justification for remarriage. The doorway to reconciliation with the separated spouse must be kept open.

But for Diana there seems no hope of reconciliation. Is Diana to wait, hoping for Hank's conversion? Hoping for a transformation that would change his values and his character? Hoping that somehow the memories of their past life and the patterns they built up relating to each other can be washed away, and that they can have a start that's fresh and new? And what if Hank marries someone else? Is Diana still to wait?

Doorway to remarriage

If we were living in Old Testament times there would be no difficulty in answering these questions. There would be no problem! Then, divorce was understood to be a doorway to remarriage. In fact, the very idea of "divorce" was such that remarriage was *expected!*

Deuteronomy, one of the books of Law in the Old Testament, puts it this way:

> When a man takes a wife and marries her, if then she finds no favor in his eyes because he has found some indecency in her, and he writes her a bill of divorce and puts it in her hand and sends her out of his house, and

she departs out of his house, and if she goes and becomes another man's wife, and the latter husband dislikes her and writes her a bill of divorce and puts it in her hand and sends her out of his house, or if the latter husband dies, who took her to be his wife, then her former husband, who sent her away, may not take her again to be his wife. . . .—Deuteronomy 24:1–4, RSV

So the Old Testament Law did establish a divorce procedure (giving a bill of divorce) and it was expected that a divorced person would remarry. The one restriction placed on the remarriage was that a divorced couple were not to remarry *each other* if one had married a third party in the meantime.

Deuteronomy does add one other restriction on divorce. If a man falsely accuses his new wife of immorality, or if rape precedes the marriage, divorce is not permitted (Deut. 22:13–19, 28–29). Beyond this, while divorce and remarriage are not encouraged, neither is denied under Old Testament Law.

In fact, in Old Testament times, the debate never focused on the question of remarriage. It was assumed that remarriage would follow a divorce. What the rabbis debated was the grounds for divorce. Some said only marital unfaithfulness was grounds. Others differed. They argued that if adultery were committed, the Law prescribed stoning to death (Deut. 22:22–24). Clearly grounds for divorce must be something other than adultery! And so this group stressed irreconcilable conflicts in the marriage, building on the phrase "finds no favor in his eyes" in Deuteronomy 24:1.

We can understand why the more liberal view was resisted. Then, as now, marriage was the foundation of the social order. Then, as now, believers viewed marriage as the first human institution ordained by God. So the importance and the sanctity of marriage must be upheld. And how could this be if society ac-

Remarriage

cepted a "cheap divorce" as an escape from the slightest discomfort?

This same fear underlies much debate about remarriage today. We fear that if we accept remarriage as legitimate, everyone will hurry to get a divorce! The fear is understandable. And the desire to uphold and strengthen marriage is commendable. But in our fear we may close our hearts to people like Diana with deep hurts and needs. In our fear we may do serious harm to the many, many Christians who today are living with spouses who were not their first. Before we too quickly lift our standards and state as irrevocable our new laws, we must be sure that our pronouncements are in harmony with the spirit and the letter of Scripture. We must be sure that what we teach is really what God intends.

If we were living in Old Testament times, we would have a very simple answer for Diana. You are divorced? Then you are free. Free to remarry, for remarriage is undoubtedly legitimate.

Misuse of divorce

The giving of any freedom is dangerous. Freedom can always be misused. It's the same with the Old Testament provision for divorce and remarriage. Some were sure to abuse the privilege.

In the time of Malachi, near the end of the Old Testament period, the prophet wrote to point out the unfaithfulness of the people to God. They brought crippled animals to the temple for sacrifice. They complained about the "burden" of a worship which God intended to be joy. They permitted social injustice and oppressed the widows and fatherless. And older men divorced their wives to marry younger, more attractive women. They were not seeking divorces with great reluctance only as a final resort. Instead they cast off faithful companions simply to feed selfish desires. God's words, recorded in Malachi, tell us clearly God's attitude toward this misuse of Law's provision for divorce:

A detestable thing has been committed in Israel and in Jerusalem: Judah has desecrated the sanctuary the Lord loves, by marrying the daughter of a foreign god. . . .

Another thing you do: You flood the Lord's altar with tears. You weep and wail because he no longer pays attention to your offerings or accepts them with pleasure from your hands. You ask, "Why?" It is because the Lord is acting as the witness between you and the wife of your youth, because you have broken faith with her, though she is your partner, the wife of your marriage covenant.

Has not the Lord made them one? In flesh and spirit they are his. And why one? Because he was seeking godly offspring. So guard yourself in your spirit, and do not break faith with the wife of your youth.

"I hate divorce," says the Lord God of Israel, "and I hate a man's covering himself with violence as well as with his garment," says the Lord Almighty. So guard yourself in your spirit, and do not break faith.—Malachi 2:11, 13–16

Anyone who has gone through a divorce, or who knows others who are experiencing one, has some understanding of why God hates divorce. They know the agony as two lives that have been linked so intimately are torn apart. They know the sense of rejection and hopelessness, the guilt and the shaming sense of worthlessness that accompany the trauma. God's goal in giving marriage to man was to build, not to tear down. To create a supportive union, not destructive isolation. And no divorce can avoid just this kind of anguish.

God, who loves us deeply, does hate divorce. For our sakes. If in the Old Testament God permitted divorce, and built that provision into Scripture's revelation of his will, it can only be because at times there can be greater hurt, greater damage to persons, by remaining married than by divorcing.

But divorce is never to be lightly undertaken. The provision of divorce can never be seen as a license for easy separation. God's ideal remains a simple one. That ideal is the faithfulness of a married couple to each other and faithfulness to the promise of oneness that was entered into as a Covenant witness by God.

2

Do Not Break Faith

Don stood on the driveway as Susan opened the car door and turned to get in. They stood there, just looking at each other. Then Don reached out and gently cupped Sue's face in his hands.

"I love you, Susan."

Tears came to her eyes. "Thanks, Don."

Then she turned quickly, slipped into the driver's seat and started the car. In a moment she was gone. Forever.

Don and Susan were a Christian couple with a good marriage. She's called it a "90 percent marriage" when she told Don she was leaving him to marry an acquaintance. Somehow the 90 percent marriage wasn't enough for Susan. She had to have 100 percent. And she felt she could never have that total fulfillment she yearned for with Don.

The winter months in the big house Don had bought for Susan and their two children were the hardest time in Don's life. More than once in the loneliness he thought of simply placing his head in the oven and turning on the gas. More than once he hurled himself outside to pace across the Minnesota hills when fears about the kids tore at his imagination.

Don knew the agony of divorce all too well. But he had been helpless. It was Susan who made the choice.

When the Bible speaks so firmly and says to married couples, "do not break faith," we know that Scripture is speaking in terms of choice. It is possible to reject the words and go the way Susan chose. But it is also possible to choose a lifestyle of faithfulness that can redeem a marriage.

The picture of that lifestyle of faithfulness is given in teachings of Jesus that led up to his most significant statement on divorce. It's important for us to grasp what Jesus was saying both as an option for anyone considering divorce and as background for the New Testament's divorce teaching.

Events began to unfold when, as recorded in Matthew 18:1, Jesus' disciples came to him and asked, "Who is the greatest in the kingdom of heaven?" (RSV). All the dialogue and the events recorded in the next three chapters of Matthew's Gospel focus on this issue. Greatness. How do we *achieve* it in our relationship with a God who does rule over the world of men?

Jesus did not answer their question at first. Instead, he called to a child. When the child came, Jesus rested his hands on the child's shoulders and faced the twelve. "Unless you change and become like little children, you will never enter the kingdom of heaven. . . . whoever humbles himself like this child is the greatest in the kingdom of heaven" (Matt. 18:3–4). For months stretching into years Jesus had called the people of Israel to him. But they had held back and had pondered and hesitated. Not "this child." He had responded without question to the call of Jesus. He had "humbled himself" in the sense of surrendering his will to Christ and acting on the Master's words.

This is the beginning, and the end, of spiritual achievement. To hear, and to respond, to the voice of God.

But immediately Jesus went on. He warned His listeners against causing these "little ones" to sin. The open, responsive and humble quality must be nurtured and encouraged. Jesus then gave three stories which show how his "little ones" can live together to achieve this kind of greatness.

Like sheep

The first story Jesus told (Matt. 18:10–14) illustrated the precept, "See that you do not look down on one of these little ones." It's the story of a shepherd with a hundred sheep. One wanders away. In deep concern the shepherd leaves the ninety-nine and goes in search of the lost one. When he finds it, his only emotion is one of joy. "I tell you the truth," Jesus put it, "he is happier about that one sheep than about the ninety-nine that did not wander off."

Often in the Bible human beings are spoken of as sheep. "All we like sheep," Isaiah the prophet says, "have gone astray; we have turned every one to his own way"(53:6, RSV). There is something of the wanderer in the nature of sheep, and of men. We tend to turn aside from the right path.

But what do we do when a *person* goes astray? The shepherd, who represents God in these tales of lost sheep, goes to seek him or her out. The Shepherd recognizes the sin, but does not let wandering threaten the relationship. Instead he takes the initiative to seek out the lost wanderer in hopes of restoring him. When restoration takes place, there is room only for joy.

When my oldest son was two, I remember him toddling full speed toward a busy street. I ran after him, snatched him up, and hugged him to me with joy. Somehow it's much harder when children are older. Or when it's a wife or husband who has strayed in the relationship. Then we sometimes feel a self-righteous pride in "taking them back" when they return. All too often we feel justified in reminding him or her of past failure.

After all, the straying of a loved one hurts. We feel we have a right to anger. A right to condemn. A right to make him pay just a little for pain he caused.

Jesus' words remind us that each of us "little ones" is very much like a sheep. So prone to stray. So likely to wander. But a person who has wandered from a healthy relationship must not be looked down on or condemned. Such a person still has worth and value. Such a person is to be sought out and restored, and when restoration comes the joy of it is to wash the bitterness and the anger and the desire for revenge from our hearts.

Like family

Next Jesus turns to the family to guide us (Matt. 18:15–17). He speaks of a brother sinning against us, and urges us to go to a brother when this happens. We are to openly show our hurt and confront him about the hurting action. This loving confrontation is to be pursued even by inviting others in to witness and mediate. Reconciliation and the healing of hurts are this important.

Peter the Apostle understood Jesus to be counseling forgiveness. Tugging on Jesus' sleeve, Peter asked, "Lord, how many times shall I forgive my brother when he sins against me? Up to seven times?" (18:21).

Peter was making a generous offer. It's possible he even expected commendation. Peter, like the rest of us, understood that it's easy to forgive a person who apologizes the first time he asks.

"Sorry I was late, Madge. I got caught in traffic."

"That's okay, Ted. It's just that I was worried about you." A quick smile, the warm touch of a hand, and the lateness is forgotten as well as forgiven. Each is secure in the assurance of the other's love.

But what if lateness is a pattern? What if Ted's repeated apologies seem more and more mocking? Soon Madge is going to feel hurt. "If he really cared about how I feel, he'd at least make an effort," Madge thinks. And a seed of bitterness is planted, growing quietly with each repeated incident.

Jesus' answer was not the one Peter expected. "I tell you, not seven times, but seventy-seven times." That answer was clear, and the idiom understood. What Jesus states is *unlimited forgiveness.* It is the extension to our loved one of a new start again and again and again, as long as a fresh start is required.

To understand this we need to grasp something of the Bible's concept of forgiveness. The root words in both Old and New Testament languages mean "to send away." And they refer to sin: to the wrong act or fault which actually caused the hurt and sense of alienation. When God deals with human sin in forgiveness, he does not simply deal with guilt feelings, nor does he say, in effect, "Think nothing of it. It's not important." No, God deals with the reality of sin and in forgiveness "sends away" that sin. "As far as the east is from the west," the Old Testament declared, "so far does he remove our transgressions from us" (Ps. 103:12, RSV). This *removal of sin* by the forgiving act of God is at the heart of Scripture's teaching about the relationship between God and man. God's love for us impelled him to send Jesus Christ into our universe to suffer death, because only by such a radical act could God be free to remove our sin. Thus Hebrews 10:17 quotes God as saying: "I will remember their sins and their misdeeds no more" (RSV). Forgiven sin is *gone,* so completely dealt with by God that it is as if it never happened. Even God cannot call to mind forgiven sin.

There is another word translated "forgive" in the New Testament. It is *choridzomai,* which means "be gracious to." It is a word that is applied to one individual's forgiveness of another. You and I cannot "send away" the sin of another person in the sense of removing it. Only God can give that kind of forgiveness. But what we can do, and are to do, is to deal with each other *graciously.* When sin comes and hurts are felt, we are to model our attitude on God's, and share the hurt with our loved one so that forgiveness can be extended and received.

In every family there are sure to be hurts and sins. Even when we love sincerely we will make mistakes, or be thoughtless and insensitive. And in times of anger we may strike out with a desire to wound. At such times God has given us a pattern for healing. We are to open our hearts to our husband or wife, share the hurt, and lavishly spend ourselves in the kind of forgiveness that forgets the past and remains ever new through the giving of a fresh start.

Like servants

This extension of unlimited forgiveness seems almost an impossible expectation. How can a mere human being find the freedom to keep on forgiving even repeated hurts?

Jesus' next story explains. It is the story of a servant whose King called him to settle his debts (Matt. 18:21–35). He owed, in our money, about ten million dollars. And he could not pay. In tears he begged the King to give him time to pay. Moved to pity, the King "canceled the debt and let him go." In the story Jesus then follows the forgiven servant. As he walks he meets a fellow servant who owes him a debt of just a few dollars. Angered when his fellow servant is unable to pay, the first servant attacks and chokes him, finally having the man thrown into debtors' prison.

Then the other servants reported the incident to the King. Furious, the King recalled his servant. "You wicked servant," he thundered. "I canceled all that debt of yours because you begged me to. Shouldn't you have had mercy on your fellow servant just as I had on you?" (18:32–33).

As in many of the stories Jesus told, the characters represented God and men. God is the King, to whom a great debt is owed. But God is the kind of Person who has a deep compassion for his servants. Thus when the first servant begged for time to pay the unimaginable debt, the King went beyond his request. He canceled the debt! In essence, Jesus taught that God is not willing to build his relationship with us on the basis of moral obligation. Instead, God places worth and value on the individual as a person. And God seeks a relationship with us based on forgiveness, not works.

But then how shall we live as a forgiven people? Shall we establish in our relationships with each other that system of "rights" and "obligations" that God himself set aside when he forgave us for Jesus' sake? Jesus' argument is clear. It is because you are forgiven that you should have mercy on your fellow servants just as God has had on you!

These three stories, and the lifestyle they portray, are important to all believers who want to understand spiritual greatness. But they are especially important to married couples. They tell the married that we live in an imperfect world. Our spouses will at times wander from the way of love. There will be thoughtlessness and selfishness that hurt us deeply. And our spouses

Remarriage

will sin against us. Cruel and bitter things will be said. Actions will be taken that are meant to hurt.

We can store up these hurts and let bitterness grow. We can take our own subtle kinds of revenge to hurt in return. We can demand our "rights" as a husband or wife to consideration and to love. But these attitudes will only drive us farther apart.

Or we can realize that we live in a world that is still imperfect. We can make the choice to value our spouses anyway, and we can deal with the hurts that will come in the way Jesus outlined. We can discover the joy of reconciliations. We can know the freedom of extending unlimited forgiveness, because we know in our relationship with God that we too need, and have received, the healing that forgiveness gives.

Susan and Don

Don had been a good husband and a loving father. Even Susan had to rate him "90 percent." Don was and is a mature Christian and a loving man.

But Susan couldn't bear to live in the reality of our world. Romantically she yearned for the ideal: for the "100 percent marriage." Susan had never realized that God's way of building people together is not only through a series of shared joys, but also through a series of shared trials.

It takes hurting and being hurt, forgiving and being forgiven, to grow to oneness in marriage.

Susan didn't *have to* remember the things that had gone wrong or that had disappointed her. Susan could have let God's forgiveness flow through her to her husband, and as she did she would have found the memories of the hard times growing dim.

But Susan made her choice.

And her choice was to break faith.

Her choice was an unnecessary divorce, and a remarriage that, with her idealized image of marriage, is bound to disappoint.

Her choice is one evidence of the impact of sin on the world in which we live and on the personalities of us all.

3

"Is It Lawful?"

Jesus has just finished his description of the greatness lifestyle. As he travels, he is approached by several Pharisees who come to test him. They ask, "Is it lawful to divorce one's wife for any cause?" (Matt. 19:3, RSV).

The Pharisees were a small group in Israel of deeply committed men. Their name means "separated," and many debate whether the name came from their careful separation from everything non-Jewish or from their desire to "divide" the Scriptures to understand all that God required. Whatever their name may mean, these men had earned the respect of the Hebrew people. They were openly, vocally, and unequivocally committed to God's Law, which they understood to mean both the writings we know as the Old Testament and the traditional interpretations of the Scriptures which had built up over the centuries.

When the Pharisees asked "Is it lawful?" they were asking the question that was to them the most important question of all. To the Pharisees "Law" summed up their whole existence. They lived for the Law, for they thought of Law as the one avenue to greatness in the eyes of God.

But Jesus did not answer their question! Instead of turning to Law, Christ went back in the Scriptures to the original Creation. "Haven't you read," he asked, "that at the beginning the Creator 'made them male and female,' and said, 'For this reason a man will leave his father and mother and be united to his wife, and the two will become one flesh'? So they are no longer two, but one. Therefore what God has joined together, let man not separate" (19:4–6).

The Pharisees were not pleased with this restatement of the Divine ideal. They would not be turned aside from their concern for Law. "Why then . . . did Moses command that a man give his wife a certificate of divorce and send her away?"

Jesus' reply was stunning. "Moses permitted you to divorce your wives because your hearts were hard. But it was not this way from the beginning. I tell you that anyone who divorces his wife, except for marital unfaithfulness, and marries another woman commits adultery" (vv. 7–9).

The way of Law

Before we explore the impact of this bombshell teaching of Jesus on our study of remarriage, it's important to see what Jesus was saying to the Pharisees. He was not primarily making a statement about marriage. Jesus was making a statement about Law.

The Old Testament Law was given late in mankind's history. Generations lived and died without its guidance. It was only some 1,400 years before Christ, when Israel flowed as an unruly mob out of Egypt toward freedom, that Law was introduced. The need for Law is illustrated by the reactions of the Israelites as God led them away from Egypt into the wilderness. At the first hint of a problem, the people murmured and complained, even to the point of planning to stone Moses who led them. So God led them to Mount Sinai. There, as the mountain shook and thunder and lightning evidenced God's holy presence, this undisciplined people vowed to obey a Law that God would give them. That Law would guide the details of their social and religious life. Their criminal code and ethical standards would be prescribed. By building a society guided by the Law, the people of Israel would be able to demonstrate through their community as well as their individual characters something of the moral character of their God.

All Israelites held a deep reverence for the Law. Moses was the Lawgiver. God himself had handed Moses the tablets of stone. Angels had been mediators of other details of the pact between God and his people. Surely the Law was the highest expression of holiness possible. Surely a human being could only achieve greatness by total commitment to every detail of Law's expression of the Divine will.

This was the core of the Pharisees' faith. Law is highest. Law is all.

But Jesus had gone back beyond the Law, and had stated an ideal expressed in the Creation story. God created human sexuality and his purpose was that two persons, a man and woman, might establish a permanent and unbreakable union. If God had permitted divorce in the Law, that permission was only given because of the hardness of human hearts.

What was Jesus showing the Pharisees about Law? It was something even his disciples did not yet see. *Rather than being the highest of all standards, the Law was evidence that God is willing to accommodate his ideal to the sinfulness of man.* Rather than being a way to achieve greatness, Law was a constant reminder of human failure. Rather than a spur to greater struggles, Law was a revelation of God's compassionate understanding of men and society warped by the existence of sin. How tragic then the Pharisees' misuse of Law. How tragic, because in their insistent examination of every detail they had lost sight of the God who stood behind the Law, and who had shown himself willing to love and accept those who fell short.

The new legalism

The disciples failed to understand Jesus' point. They jumped to the conclusion that in answering the Pharisees Jesus was stating a new and higher law. That Jesus was laying a new and heavier demand on his people.

Frightened, they reacted. "If this is the situation between a husband and wife, it is better not to marry" (Matt. 19:10). If Jesus were truly cutting off the possibility of divorce, how much better not to risk entry into a relationship that would be without exit!

Today as well, sincere disciples of Jesus jump to the same conclusion. They see Christ's restatement of the marital ideal as an unalterable command. To them there can be no possibility of divorce entertained. And, if someone should sin so greatly as to divorce, remarriage is unthinkable. For Jesus clearly seems to say that remarriage involves adultery.

But is Jesus giving us a new, higher, and more perfect law? Or is Jesus, who sought to help the Pharisees look beyond Law to understand God's will, also inviting us to see the realities of marriage and divorce in some nonlegal light?

Certainly Jesus' response to his disciples' worried objection doesn't suggest the laying down of a new law. "Not everyone can accept this teaching," Jesus said (19:11). He went on to point out that some human beings were able to choose celibate lives, some even renouncing marriage for the sake of the kingdom of heaven. But the married state is the norm for most of us. After all, it was God himself who created us male and female. It was God who designed sex, and who in his wisdom shaped into sexuality our deep need to love and be loved, to warm and be warmed, to give and to receive in this most intimate of relationships. No, Jesus went on, aluding to the principle he had stated about marriage as an ideal rather than as a law, "The one who can accept this should accept it." And he left forever open the options of the person who simply cannot.

The next incident in the flow of the Bible passage is conclusive. Matthew 19:13–14 records, "Then little children were brought to Jesus for him to place his hands on them and pray for them. But the disciples rebuked those who brought them. Jesus said, 'Let the little children come to me, and do not hinder them, for the kingdom of heaven belongs to such as these.'" What is the significance of that incident? Simply this: In the Old Testament system, an individual came under Law, and was responsible to Law, only at age twelve. The "little children" Jesus identified as owners of his kingdom simply did not relate to God through Law! Even the Pharisees would recognize this. Law never touched the life or the relationship with God of anyone who was a "little child."

The wrong question

The great tragedy of the legal approach to divorce and remarriage is the tragedy of all legalism. It tears our attention from the human issues involved.

One time these same Pharisees went to the synagogue on the Sabbath to hear Jesus teach. Matthew 12:10 indicates a man with a shriveled hand was there. Cunningly they watched to see what Jesus would do.

Would he perform an act of healing on the Sabbath? To the Pharisees such an act would be "work," and Jesus would show himself to be a Sabbath breaker!

But Jesus knew their thoughts. He had just an hour or so before said to them, "If you had known what these words mean, 'I desire mercy, not sacrifice,' you would not have condemned the innocent" (12:7). And when one of the Pharisees asked him, "Is it lawful to heal on the Sabbath?" Jesus was ready. Matthew records what Jesus said and did:

> "What man of you, if he has one sheep and it falls into a pit on the sabbath, will not lay hold of it and lift it out? Of how much more value is a man than a sheep! So it is lawful to do good on the sabbath." Then he said to the man, "Stretch out your hand." And the man stretched it out, and it was restored, whole like the other. But the Pharisees went out and took counsel against him, how to destroy him.—12:11–14, RSV

Once again they had asked the wrong question—"Is it lawful?" And Jesus had shown that something that might not be technically legal could still be lawful, in fullest harmony with Law's intent, if it were "to do good." God's heart desired mercy, not sacrifice.

The Pharisees at the synagogue showed no compassion for the cripple. They used him, mocking his disability. Their only concern was to trap Jesus in words and interpretations so that he might be accused. But again Jesus' actions had cut through to the heart of the issue, and because Jesus had shown them to be a pious but merciless people, the Pharisees hated him enough to kill.

How then about divorce and remarriage? If "Is it lawful?" is the wrong question, what is the right question?

The right question is this: Is there any way to heal

the hurt of broken commitments? Is there any way to restore shattered hopes and fan the ashes of love? And to this question Jesus has already given his answer! Yes!

Yes, there is a way. It is the way of greatness, the way of living with each other as little ones. Healing can be found as we set aside anger and are reconciled to our loved ones with joy. Healing can come as we bring our hurts into the open, and let forgiveness wash away the bitterness and pain. Healing can come as we extend to others the forgiveness we have received from God.

This is the right question. Not, "Is it lawful?" But, "Is there healing?"

But the Pharisees did not ask the right question. And all too often we fail to ask that question ourselves. We too become bound in our legalism. We debate divorce and decry remarriage and become insensitive to the broken hearts of those to whom God would hold out hope. Mercy. And not sacrifice. This is the way of Christ.

Don and Susan are divorced now. She has remarried. Don is planning to marry, too. If the right question had been asked in time by Susan, this couple might have avoided the agony of their divorce.

But it's too late for Don to deal with what might have been. Don now has to live the rest of his life with the wrong question: "Is it lawful?"

This is the question that Christians will ask. The question that many will answer with a simple, blunt word: "No!" With no thought of mercy or the role of mercy in God's plan for a shattered humanity, they will retreat in their understanding of what the Bible says, and they will conclude "no remarriage." Oh, they will be kind enough. They'll tell Don that the divorce was not his fault, so he is still acceptable. But they'll also tell him that God's Law is clear. If he should remarry, he will definitely step beyond the revealed will of God. He will sin. And he will step beyond the range of their forgiveness and their acceptance as well.

4

Because Your Hearts Were Hard

Marilyn sat in the office crying. She'd come for help, but it was her own conscience, not the man across the desk, which condemned her.

Not that Marilyn was what we've come to call the "guilty party." Not in a way.

Marilyn had filed for her divorce, but only after it was certain that Jack would never come back to her. She loved her husband. But even more than that she felt morally bound to seek a reconciliation. There had been things she'd done that had bothered Jack. There must have been! A man didn't just leave his wife and children for no cause at all.

So she'd followed Jack and his friend Carl into the bars they went to. With tears in her eyes she'd even pled in public for Jack to come back. And when her husband laughed . . . and Carl tittered . . . she'd swallowed the stabbing hurt and tried again.

Then Jack left her—for good, he'd said—and took a room with Carl. But she kept on trying. God knows she tried. Even when all her friends whispered and shook their heads in sympathy, Marilyn tried. Finally one of them came right out and said it. "Marilyn, for pity's sake! Don't you know your husband's a homosexual?"

Marilyn actually went to Jack and asked him. Was he really "living with" Carl? Jack just laughed, and in a nasty tone of voice said, "That's for me to know and you to find out."

When the divorce finally came, she still hadn't admitted the truth. She still wondered what it was she'd done to drive Jack away. How had she failed as a woman that Jack had turned to . . . that?

Like the other people in this book, Marilyn is a real person. And her story really happened. *Marilyn* is not her name, of course. But *she* is real. And what she and the others experienced is repeated over and over again in literally thousands of homes across our country.

Just as they have been repeated since the beginning of time.

In the beginning

In responding to the Pharisees' question about the lawfulness of divorce, Jesus went back to the original Creation. He stated God's ideal, the Divine intention for the marriage relationship. To understand the rest of what Jesus is saying, we need to go back to that same early time. For the other pivotal point of Jesus' argument, "your hearts were hard," also finds its roots in the Garden of Eden and in the experiences of Adam and Eve.

We remember that account well. After an idyllic time in Eden, lived in the closest of fellowship with God and each other, Adam and Eve failed a critical test. They ate from a tree whose fruit had been forbidden by God.

It's important for us to see that the planting of that

tree in the center of the Garden was a positive act on the part of God, not a negative one. Human beings were created for full fellowship with God. The Westminster Catechism says it well: we were created "to glorify God, and to enjoy him forever." To have fellowship with God, there had to be a correspondence. This is why God created us in his image and likeness—so that qualities of our personhood could resonate with his. He gave us a mind, that we might understand and explore and discover and create. He gave us emotions, that we might share with him experiences of joy and exaltation, of compassion and care, of anger and sorrow. But if we were to truly share with God all that it means to be a person, we must also be given the gift of choice. There must be an opportunity to exercise our will, that our choice to love and obey God might have meaning. Where there were no alternatives, there could be no meaning in choosing the good.

So the placement of that tree was a good gift. It lifted Adam and Eve beyond other created beings and gave them a freedom and responsibility that man would otherwise never have known.

But with the freedom came danger. With the opportunity to choose good came the possibility of choosing evil.

And Eve, then Adam, did make that wrong choice. They exercised their freedom to sin.

And the whole creation has suffered from that choice because we all, from that time, have participated in it.

Sin's impact

Reading the story of the Fall in the early chapters of Genesis, we hear God warn the two: "The day that thou eatest thereof thou shalt surely die" (Gen. 2:17, KJV). The day they ate, they did not seem to die. They continued in the garden for a time. They lived long lives. But God's word of warning had not been empty. The New Testament says that through their act of sin "death passed upon all men" (Rom. 5:12, KJV).

The immediate history of the race helps us see what death, in its spiritual sense, means. Adam and Eve had two sons. One, in anger, murdered the other. This murderer established a society and culture that expressed over and over again the mark of death. In Genesis 4:23 we see two early evidences of sin's distortion. Lamech, one of Cain's descendants, recalled his own murder of another by saying, "I have slain a man for wounding me, a young man for striking me" (RSV). Surely if Cain killed without provocation, Lamech argued, revenge justified his own act of murder. And Lamech, Scripture says, took two women as wives. The pattern of the ideal was broken, as sin hardened the hearts and the perceptions of mankind.

Looking through both Scripture and secular history we find repeated evidence of the impact of sin. No society has ever existed in which strife and injustice were not found. Discriminatory laws, crime, warfare, oppression, slavery . . . age after age the same bitter fruit is found ripening on humanity's tree.

"There is none righteous," says the prophet, quoted in Romans 3:10 (KJV). "There is none that doeth good, no, not one."

Every society, every individual, has been touched and warped by the existence of sin.

While we can't recognize it now, the Bible tells us that the whole creation was affected. Weeds sprang up to choke out crops. Nature twisted in a new kind of bondage. We cannot hear the stones cry out, perhaps, but the Bible says that "the creation was subjected to futility, not of its own will but by the will of him who subjected it in hope; because the creation itself will be set free from its bondage to decay and obtain the glorious liberty of the children of God" (Rom. 8:20–21, RSV).

It is against the background of this reality that Jesus explained God's permission of divorce and remarriage. "It was because your hearts were hard." It was because sin's impact on you, on your society, on creation itself, was so tragically real that something less than the ideal was authorized by God.

It is very important to think carefully here. Jesus did not say in any way that God had lowered his ideal. Jesus did not say that divorce and remarriage are *right*. In fact, in going back before Law to the Creation Jesus demonstrated conclusively that divorce and remarriage have *never been* "right"!

In making his pronouncement in Matthew 19, Jesus was not adding something new to the Law. He was affirming a reality that had always been true, from the Creation on through the age of Law and now as well.

But still God permitted divorce! God allowed the certificate of divorce to be drawn up, witnessed, and presented to a spouse. It was God who spoke of the individual's remarriage after the divorce.

It was God who gave the "sin" of divorce and remarriage its social legitimacy.

Why?

Because God understood the "hardness of heart" that sin's existence causes. God understood the dilemma faced by innocent people like Diana and Don and Marilyn. God understood that in a sin-tainted human society, many men and women would not follow the path to greatness, and that for some the hurt would be too great to bear.

Jesus' statement about man's hardness of heart is not a statement of condemnation. It is a statement of compassion and mercy. Knowing our need, God showed himself willing to meet us in the reality of our lives, coming to us with grace. He did not demand that we meet him only in that storied and desirable land of the ideal.

Sin

The topic of sin is never a pleasant one. But something that affects our lives so greatly should be understood better than it often is. For sin is both a condition and an act.

On the one hand Scripture says "sin is the transgression of the law" (1 John 3:4, KJV). On the other hand, sin is described as a principle living in and with us, warping us against our will (Rom. 7:16–25).

The biblical words for sin reflect this same duality. One set of Old Testament words pictures sin as rebellion: conscious acts willfully taken against what we know to be right. Another set of Old Testament words portrays sin as falling short: missing the mark in spite of our best efforts to hit the target God has set before us. The New Testament words carry the same meanings.

Willful sin involves the *choice* of wrong. But the other kind of sin throws us into a different turmoil. The other kind of sin forces us to suffer the effects of what we have not chosen. We suffer for what we are . . . and for what others around us are.

Listen to Paul's words in Romans 7. We can hear an echo of our own anguish, and feel with Marilyn the agony of that betrayal of her ideals, the sin which she did not choose, but for which she still blames herself.

I can will what is right, but I cannot do it. For I do not do the good I want, but the evil I do not want is what I do. . . .
For I delight in the law of God, in my inmost self,

but I see in my members another law at war with the law of my mind and making me captive to the law of sin which dwells in my members.—Romans 7:18–19, 22–23, RSV

These words help us see that God was willing to compromise his ideal, and to legitimize marriage and divorce, not to lower his standards, but to reach out and heal casualties in the war against sin.

Consistency

God has always had one basic way of dealing with human failure. That way is to come alongside us with the gift of forgiveness and by his healing touch bring the possibility of health and growth.

Man's way of dealing with human failure is different. Our way is to retreat to the safety of legislation. Legalism gives us a wall behind which to hide as we condemn those we have placed on the outside. Legalism gives us a platform on which to stand so we can feel taller than those we place below us. Legalism gives us a weapon with which to strike out and punish others for the failures that we ourselves fear.

This is especially true in the area of divorce and remarriage. We forgive the adulterer in our churches much more quickly than we forgive the woman who has suffered the abandonment of divorce, or the man who has chosen to remarry. We welcome the converted murderer to our pulpits and lionize the reformed purveyor of smut. But somehow we feel it is only right that lifelong suffering result for anyone who has been involved in any way in the one unforgivable sin of our day.

How strange.

How strange that for every other sin we recognize a grace in God that promises forgiveness and restoration. For every other sin we believe that the past can be wiped out and a fresh new start given. But in the sole case of divorce and remarriage we believe that God abandons his own consistency. That he holds the stern, unyielding position that only one opportunity can be given. And if sin in one or both of the partners should lead to a divorce, both guilty and innocent must pay for that failure for the rest of their lives.

How strange, particularly when Jesus himself shows that it was God who gave legitimacy to remarriage in Old Testament days! And that God did so because he recognized that the hardness of our sin-warped hearts would make achievement of his ideal impossible for some.

Jack's perversion is another expression of our hardness of heart. His was the active choice of rebellious sin. Marilyn's tears were also an expression of mankind's hardness of heart. Hers was an unwilling participation. But it was a participation that was very real.

Today Marilyn still cries. She torments herself with feelings of guilt. And at night she cries because she believes that God has firmly closed off to her any possibility of ever being loved again.

Is the God who accommodated himself to our hardness of heart in the age of Law now, in the age of grace, untouched by Marilyn's misery? Or is remarriage still an option for people like her? Is remarriage still, as it was in Old Testament times, *legitimate?* Can we believe that God will actively lead Marilyn into a new marriage relationship?

5

From the Beginning

Marriage was a golden ideal to Linda. And she was going to marry a man who would become a minister!

Linda yearned so much to experience the ideal. Her mother was an insensitive person; her dad simply seemed weak. Linda grew up feeling unloved, and with deep doubts about her own worth. But marriage would change all that. In marriage, her wonderful husband to be would make her into a new woman. She often felt so angry—about her mom and dad, about the women at the office where she worked, about her life in general. But when she was married, then she'd be able to love.

Linda wanted to love, even though she felt she couldn't. She felt a little guilty about that. She couldn't even love the man she was going to marry. But he would help her learn to love. He was spiritually strong. And she'd draw strength from him. Together they'd experience God's ideal.

Two decades later the dream of the ideal was gone for Linda. Her husband had failed her. He talked about love. But he hadn't done what she had so desperately needed. He hadn't made *her* a different person.

The loss of hope has brought a kind of peace to Linda. But she feels a deep anger against her husband. Others respect and appreciate him. But *she* knows what he's really like. Every day he does things to hurt or demean her. She doesn't understand why he does things like that. Or why he doesn't show any interest in helping their girls grow spiritually. But she feeds on all the little things he does and doesn't do, and finds some consolation in reminding herself whenever she feels the emptiness, "It's not my fault. He's never loved me as he *should* have."

Linda will probably never know what the psychiatrist told her husband: "Your wife is a paranoid personality, with a substantial amount of hostility directed toward you. It's derived, ultimately, from her childhood home and her inadequate concept of herself.

"Basically she denies any responsibility for her own feelings and for the relationship, and projects her feelings on you, interpreting whatever you do in such a way that it seems meant to hurt and punish."

Prognosis? "Characteristically, psychoses of this type tend to become stronger and stronger. I don't want to seem unspiritual, but don't set your hopes on any miracle. This is the hardest kind of thing there is to treat."

When they married, both Linda and her husband Luke held firmly to God's ideal for marriage as a oneness relationship. They held on to that ideal as the years passed. Neither one has surrendered it today. But there is no basis for expecting that either one of them will realize the ideal they each desire so strongly.

Linda and Luke are two more people who know by

agonizing personal experience what Jesus meant when he spoke of the hardness of human hearts and of failure to achieve the ideal because of sin's effect on us.

To a great extent, every ideal is like this. It is to be affirmed. It is to be desired. It is to be struggled toward. But in a sin-warped universe, it *may* not be achieved.

Let's think a bit about the marriage ideal and the goal God sets before us in the Creation account. We're told of Adam's search through the animal creation for a suitable helper. He found no one. Finally the Lord God caused a deep sleep to fall on Adam, and as he slept God took a single rib from Adam's side and from it fashioned Eve.

When God brought Eve to Adam, he immediately recognized her:

> "This at last is bone of my bones
>   and flesh of my flesh;
> she shall be called Woman,
>   because she was taken out of Man."

And Scripture adds this Divine comment: "Therefore a man leaves his father and his mother and cleaves to his wife, and they become one flesh" (Gen. 2:23–24, RSV).

Man and woman

The Jewish rabbis had a beautiful interpretation of this story. God did not take Eve from Adam's feet, so that Adam would not lord it over her. Nor from his head, that Eve might not be lifted up above him. But He took Eve from Adam's rib, that they might stand arm in arm as companions in their life on earth.

There *is* significance in the details of the Creation story. As a later creation, some might argue that Eve was inferior to Adam, and thus women as a class are inferior to men. This notion of inferiority all too easily creeps into human society as it is! But God guarded against this misunderstanding of male/female identities. He took a rib from Adam, and shaped Eve from Adam's essence. When Adam saw her he recognized the essential identity: "This is bone of my bones, and flesh of my flesh." Man and woman stand together before the Lord as fully human, as full participants together in the image and likeness of God.

This identity of man with woman is very important. God made humankind as persons, to correspond with his own attributes of personhood. Intellect, emotion, will—each must find a correspondence if there is to be fellowship and sharing. Now God has given Adam a companion who shares that identity with him! God made man and woman alike so that they could participate together in all that life on earth holds and share with each other common experiences that would blend the two into one.

Actually, the promise "they two shall be one flesh," speaks of far more than the sexual act. In the Hebrew world, life in the "flesh" was seen as our total experience in the physical universe. That is, the word *flesh* lacks the negative theological overtones of the New Testament term, and instead expresses a viewpoint. "They become one flesh" means that their lives, as lived on earth, will be bound up together in every respect. They will share themselves physically. They will share themselves emotionally. They will share themselves intellectually. They will share their values and their decisions. Through this sharing of all that they are, they will become *one.*

We can understand why this is God's ideal for us. The New Testament, when it speaks of the Church, speaks often of growth as something that comes through intimate personal relationships. "The whole body, joined and knit together by every joint with which it is supplied, when each part is working properly, makes bodily growth [from Christ, the Head] and upbuilds itself in love" (Eph. 4:16, RSV). Human beings grow and mature in a *social* context. So it is no wonder that God designed the most intimate of all possible human relationships, marriage, as a place for growth together into oneness. Together two people can become more than either one could ever be alone.

There are, of course, sexual implications in the mention of "one flesh." God created us as sexual beings. Every sensation, every thrill, every joy that a couple can know in their intimate times together were designed into our bodies and minds by the Lord himself. So in the New Testament the Apostle Paul recognizes the sexual nature of mankind, and the need for sex, as a valid motivation for marriage. Paul commends celibacy, a state he himself apparently chose. But he outlines the normal course when we warns against immorality and says:

> Each man should have his own wife and each woman her own husband. The husband should give to his wife her conjugal rights, and likewise the wife to her husband. For the wife does not rule over her own body, but the husband does; likewise the husband does not rule over his own body, but the wife does. . . . I wish that all were as I myself am. But each has his own special gift from God, one of one kind and one of another.
>
> To the unmarried and the widows I say that it is well for them to remain single as I do. But if they cannot exercise self-control, they should marry. For it is better to marry than to be aflame with passion.—1 Corinthians 7:2–4, 7–9, RSV

Marriage, then, is the coming together of two equal persons, a husband and wife, who have a shared identity as human beings shaped in the likeness and image of God. In the security of a lifelong relationship they share the totality of their lives, each confident in the commitment of the other to him or her. There is sexual joy in this relationship: the full experience of the wonderful capacities God designed into the human frame. And there is growth . . . maturing . . . transformation . . . as each ministers to the other by sharing thoughts and feelings and values and desires. In the security of total commitment, there is the possibility of growth toward the ideal for the marriage and for each individual as well. Together we are to help each other grow toward God.

Legislating the ideal?

It should be clear that achievement of this ideal, or even growth toward it, is possible only as two people work together to deepen their relationship. It is possible to legislate staying together. But it is not possible to legislate the quality of the relationship with a forced union.

God cares about the quality of the relationship. God cares about *growth* toward the ideal. *This is why God permitted divorce and remarriage in Old Testament days. God deals with reality, and the reality of some marriages then, as now, was such that harm rather than good would result to the persons involved in a legislated union.* The ideal was always held out as good and right. Failure to reach the ideal was always sin in the sense of falling short of the target which God in his goodness set before us. But God knows that ideals cannot be enforced by any Law. As the Bible says, "If a law had been given which could make alive, then righteousness would indeed be by the law" (Gal. 3:21, RSV). But neither life nor righteousness could come by Law. So God did not depend on Law as the means for enabling men to achieve the ideal!

Remarriage

Nor must *we* depend on Law. We must not depend even on the popular evangelical law of no divorce, no remarriage. Law was never meant to enable us to achieve righteousness, nor was Law meant to punish us when we don't. Law was meant to show us our need of grace, that we might turn to another way to achieve.

This is why it is actually more safe to abandon our legalistic approach to divorce and remarriage than to hold on to our prohibitions, as if they embody a new Law instituted by Jesus. God never abandons the ideal, and we must never abandon the ideal. But we will never help men and women move toward God's ideal if we depend on legislation.

No, we must return to the way of greatness. We must learn to reconcile and forgive . . . first within our own marriages. And then, if the hardness of someone's heart has so damaged a relationship that staying together will do harm rather than heal, we need to extend forgiveness to those who *must* divorce. And to those who remarry as well.

Divorce to heal

As Linda's illness deepens, Luke has been forced to consider divorce. They have not lived together as husband and wife for years now. Linda's hostility makes a sexual relationship too great a burden for her to bear, and Luke is not the kind of person who would demand his rights.

But isn't it possible that with Luke and Linda divorced, some healing might take place? Now, everything that Luke does or does not do seems to feed her illness. Could Linda function better if the burden of a marriage that is now totally distorted were removed?

As a minister, Luke knows the risk he takes. We

can forgive the ordinary man. But our spiritual leaders? No, they must be above human failures. They must be beyond the imperfection that hardness of heart has made all others subject to. And so Luke hesitates. And waits.

The ideal will never be known in his home. But will a public admission of what has in reality been a divorce, instituted by Linda years ago, destroy his ministry? Yet isn't it his duty as a husband who loves his wife as Christ loved the Church to act for *her* good, no matter what the personal cost?

This is the tension with which the Church is living in our day. How can we affirm the ideal and still deal lovingly with the real? How can we uphold the sanctity of marriage, and affirm its lifelong nature, and yet admit that there are times we need to follow the lead of God and accommodate ourselves and our ideals to the hardness of human hearts, and the distortion of lives caused by sin?

One thing is sure.

We can establish laws that demand couples like Linda and Luke stay together. But we cannot by legislation heal the hurt or change the reality of their situation. By our transmutation of an ideal into a law, we may even be guilty of the Pharisees' central sin: neglect of mercy.

We may forget that God, in his great compassion, is not afraid to meet us lovingly where we are.

Why are we afraid to follow his lead?

6

Not Everyone Can Accept

When Jesus had restated the biblical ideal in response to the Pharisee's query about Law, the disciples had objected, "If this is the situation between a man and his wife, it is better not to marry!" Who could risk a no-exit relationship?

Jesus then spoke about celibacy and about the ideal. Those who could accept celibacy might well choose this course for their lives. But not everyone can accept it. This means that most people must choose to take the risk of marriage! And it also indicates that not all will find it possible in their marriage that the Creation ideal be achieved.

So Jesus moves to the little children, whom he identifies as the citizens of his kingdom. Little children did not live under Law. And the little children who are citizens of the kingdom Jesus has established are not to relate to him or to each other through law.

In Jesus' kingdom there is a new way.

It is the way of the King.
And its name is Grace.

Grace

Grace is a very difficult concept for the human mind to master.

I remember so clearly the objections of my friends in the Navy as I told them about God's great plan of salvation by grace.

"You mean there's nothing you have to *do?*" they'd ask incredulously. And then the objections would come. "But if you know you'll be forgiven, why, you could go out and commit any sins at all!"

Their point was a simple one. This relationship based on grace and forgiveness would never work. Given the sinfulness of men, the assurance of forgiveness would simply be seen as a license to sin.

I tried to explain. I showed how, when a person became a Christian, God planted love in his or her heart. The reason a Christian doesn't run out to commit sins is that he loves God, and wants to please him. Fear of punishment simply is not the kind of motivation God relies on in dealing with his children.

Grace is like that.

Grace comes to us with forgiveness and with a promise. Grace does not threaten us, but says simply, "Love me. Let me work in your life. And I will make you a new and different person. I will lift you to be what you desperately want to be but have found that you cannot be."

Grace always seems to make ridiculous statements just like these. Grace always seems to ask us to accept the reality of our failures and our needs, inviting us to turn away from threats as motivation to choose the good and let God's love work a change within us.

Remarriage

That's why it's so difficult for us to understand grace or to live it. It goes against our perceptions of ourselves. When threat is removed, we're afraid the old in us will burst out and do its worst. We would rather rely on rules to bar us from evil than on love to guide us to good.

It is this same misunderstanding of grace we see reflected in today's fears about divorce and remarriage. "If we remove the threat of law," the feeling is, "then every married person will immediately run out and get a divorce, and remarry the first person he sees!" But when Christians turn to God, he plants love in our hearts. The Christian doesn't run out to divorce, because he loves God and wants to please him. As we love God, he operates in us and in our marriages to make us new and different persons. He operates through reconciliation and forgiveness to heal.

When we emphasize law and not grace because of our fears, we show a complete misunderstanding of the way God works to make realization of his ideal possible for his children!

The way of grace

When we come to ask how God's grace operates, we first of all discover that it operates in the world of realities. Grace is something we discover working its miracles in the real world of hardened human hearts.

And for grace to operate, it must start with our recognition and admission of sin.

Some have taught that "sinlessness" is the necessary state for fellowship with God. This is wrong. The Apostle John explains it this way:

This is the message we have heard from him and proclaim to you, that God is light and in him is no darkness at all. If we say we have fellowship with him while we walk in darkness, we lie and do not live according to the truth; but if we walk in the light, as he is in the light, we have fellowship with one another, and the blood of Jesus his Son cleanses us from all sin. If we say we have no sin, we deceive ourselves, and the truth is not in us. If we confess our sins, he is faithful and just, and will forgive our sins and cleanse us from all unrighteousness. If we say we have not sinned, we make him a liar, and his word is not in us.—1 John 1:5–10, RSV

John uses the words *light* and *darkness* in contrast here. The contrast is not one between holiness and sin, but between reality and illusion. *The Zondervan Pictorial Encyclopedia of the Bible* suggests that "light is synonymous with revelation." * As we let God's Word illuminate our understanding, we see reality as it truly is. As we reject illusions and pretense, we face ourselves and our actions and evaluate them as God does. When we walk in the light, dealing honestly and openly with the realities of our lives, then we have the possibility of fellowship with each other and the promise of fellowship with God.

How does light relate to sin? In this passage John says that any claim to be without sin is self-deceit. We are walking in darkness when we make such claims, and his truth is not in us. The "hardness of your hearts" is a fact of human existence, and when sin finds expression in our lives it must be identified and dealt with as sin.

How then does the Christian deal with sin? We appeal, John says, to the purifying blood of Jesus Christ. And "if we confess our sins, he is faithful and just, and will forgive our sins and cleanse us from all unrighteousness." This is an exciting promise. God will

---

* Merrill C. Tenney, ed., 5 vols. (Grand Rapids, MI: Zondervan Publishing House, 1975), 3:933.

meet us with forgiveness. And he will work in a purifying way in our personalities to purge unrighteousness! The remedy for sin, and the criterion for fellowship, is not sinlessness.

It is an open acknowledgment of our sins as sin and an appeal to God for forgiveness. We can be sure that with the forgiveness he will also keep on accomplishing a purifying work in our personalities.

We see from this passage how important it is for us to label sin as sin and to deal with it under God's gracious provisions. Sin that is denied stays lodged in our personalities and distorts our fellowship with God, just as it destroys our relationships with others. A discovery through revelation of God's perspective on every facet of our lives is vital if we are to have hope.

This is one reason why in Jesus' statement of the Creation ideal for marriage he went on to spell out the implications. The Pharisees depended on the Law to guide them, and so their only concern in divorce cases focused on valid reasons for a person to divorce a spouse. They viewed divorce as lawful, and therefore failed to recognize or deal with it in its relationship to sin.

Jesus would not let them live in such darkness. "I tell you that anyone who divorces his wife, except for marital unfaithfulness, [and marries another woman] commits adultery" (Matt. 5:32). Divorce and remarriage, falling so short of God's ideal, are expressions of man's hardness of heart and thus are expressions of sin. Until they are acknowledged as sin, there is no way to deal with them in terms of grace!

Grace within marriage

The first place grace may be called on to do its work is within a marriage.

Jim and Suzie had a difficult time in their marriage. Jim was uncommunicative. His life revolved around sports. And he was demanding sexually. Suzie felt more and more used by her husband. Surely he didn't value her! He spent little time with her. He never shared his thoughts or feelings. As the hurt grew, so did Suzie's resentment and desperation.

When Cary, a neighbor in the apartment complex, began to drop in to talk with her, Suzie was vulnerable. Here was someone who seemed interested in her as a person. Soon the bitterness she felt toward her husband was intensified by Jim's contrast with Cary. And all too soon Suzie, moved by "love," was giving herself to Cary with a passion she never felt with Jim.

When Jim found out he was both hurt and angry. He hadn't understood Suzie's unresponsiveness before. But to find out that she was giving freely to a stranger what she had begun to deny her own husband was more than he could stand!

When they came to the elders of their church, each was hurt and angry. Each one blamed the other for their very obvious faults, but both resisted acknowledgment of their own actions as sin. They tried to justify themselves by pointing to the faults in the partner which had "made them" do what they had done.

There was an opportunity for grace to work in their relationship. If only each had recognized sin, acknowledged it, and confessed it to the other and to God, forgiveness might have led to reconciliation. After all, as servants of a King who has forgiven us so much, we can find grace in his example to forgive each other.

And with forgiveness there is a new opportunity for fellowship and the sharing of lives.

Grace within marriage always works this way, even when the sins that have distorted the relationship have grown from the "little things" to the most serious.

But neither Jim nor Suzie would choose the way of grace. Neither one would take responsibility for their marriage failures. To Jim the situation was clear. Jesus himself had talked of "marital unfaithfulness" as a

Remarriage

basis for a divorce which permitted remarriage without the stigma of adultery. "Is that what Matthew 19 means?" Jim demanded. Hurt and angry, Jim wanted to deal with the marriage in the way "lawfully" open to him. Jim wanted, and obtained, a divorce.

Grace after divorce

In the Gospels, as in the Old Testament, divorce is assumed to be a doorway to remarriage. Whenever Jesus speaks of divorce he adds "and remarries." In some passages it sounds as if "the one divorcing" is guilty of adultery, and the "innocent party" does not share that stigma. In two passages Jesus speaks of an exception related somehow to a sexual sin which, though translated "marital unfaithfulness" in many versions, is not really understood today by any of the commentators.

But again, the Gospels and the Old Testament do seem to see divorce and remarriage as two sides of the same coin. When one divorces, it is assumed that remarriage will follow.

But then we come to a new addition in Paul's first letter to the Corinthians. Arguing from Christ's teachings in the Gospels, Paul gives the married a command: "A wife must not separate from her husband. . . . And a husband must not divorce his wife." Between these two statements is the new prescription: "But if she does, she must remain unmarried or else be reconciled to her husband" (1 Cor. 7:10, 11).

Again, we face the reality.

Divorce falls short of God's ideal, and the believer who seeks God's will is not to initiate the divorce proceeding. But in a world under the pall of human hardheartedness, divorces will at times come. So, "if she does" separate or divorce, there is to be another opportunity given for grace to work.

The divorced person is to remain unmarried or be reconciled to his or her spouse. The doorway to forgiveness and reconciliation is still to be kept open!

How gracious this is, both of God and of the separated spouse. It is gracious of God, for once again he has shown himself willing to continue to work with a person who has sinned in the matter of the divorce. It is gracious of the spouse, in that he or she still shows himself willing to accept the partner back if God works a work in the other's life that makes reconciliation possible.

Ann came to one of the elders with a request. "Tell me what to do. My ex-husband wants me to remarry him, and I don't know if I should or not."

The elder spent several hours with Ann. He listened to her story and heard all her doubts about her ex's supposed "reformation." Together they looked at passages of Scripture that might be helpful. And finally, he told Ann, "Go home now and pray about it, and ask the Lord what he wants you to do."

Ann was angry. She'd come to a spiritual leader to have him *tell* her! This advice to "pray about it" wasn't what she wanted at all.

But Ann did pray.

And the Lord showed her plainly that he did not want her to remarry her husband . . . at that time.

Ann is still living as a single person.

The doorway to reconciliation is open.

Grace after divorce is still operating in her life.

Grace in remarriage

Ted is a Sunday school teacher with a fine and growing adult class. He's divorced, and his ex-wife has remarried. As far as Ted can see, the doorway to any possible reconciliation with her is closed.

Last Sunday Ted taught his adults on the subject

of divorce and remarriage. And he announced that he was planning to remarry. Ted also shared the peace that God had given him about this decision. He is sure that God is leading him and his bride-to-be into this new marriage.

Ted was jolted by his friends' reactions. They had accepted him as a divorced man and were sure that the divorce had not been his fault. But they could not accept the idea of remarriage. "It's *wrong*," one man said angrily. "You *can't* have peace about it."

Certainly the man is right about remarriage involving "wrong." The tension in the marriage that led up to the divorce was wrong. The choice of a divorce by the couple, rather than struggling together to forgive and find healing, was wrong.

But once again we are confronted with two facts. Divorce and remarriage involved wrong in the time of Law as well. Yet God, in Scripture, instituted a divorce procedure that legitimized remarriage. As a falling short of the ideal, divorce and remarriage are sin. But certainly God's provision of divorce and remarriage options in the Old Testament indicates that he intends to deal with this sin by granting forgiveness and also the freedom to search in a new relationship for the elusive ideal.

The other fact is the fact of grace. God remembers our frame, that we are but dust, and deals with us in mercy rather than recrimination. Mercy, and grace, may well view the needs of little ones as of enough significance to permit, and even guide them into, a relationship of marriage in which those needs can be met.

If so, how in harmony this is with the loving-kindness of God! How in keeping this is with the encouraging words of the writer to the Hebrews, who reminds us, "we have not a high priest who is unable to sympathize with our weaknesses, but one who in every respect has been tempted as we are, yet without sinning. Let us then with confidence draw near to the throne of grace, that we may receive mercy and find grace to help in time of need" (4:15–16, RSV).

He is able to sympathize with our weaknesses.

We can come boldly to him.

When we do, we discover his great gifts to us in our failures and in our sins.

Mercy.

And Grace.

7

While There's Hope

So much teaching in Scripture on divorce and remarriage sounds "final." It certainly is that way with Paul's prescriptions in 1 Corinthians 7.

"A wife must not separate from her husband."

"A husband must not divorce his wife."

These phrases are so blunt and clear that we read them as exceptionless. Except that Paul immediately treats them in a different way.

"Do not."

"But if she does, she must remain unmarried or else be reconciled to her husband." With the phrase "but if she does," Paul shows us that the realities of our lives can never be fully encompassed in "final" statements. The guiding principle may be valid, and God's desire for a permanent relationship may be clear, but in a sin-hardened world the exception may still *exist.* The ideal has not changed. But the reality must be dealt with.

This is how we have to understand the whole section

in 1 Corinthians 7 that deals with questions of marriage, divorce, and remarriage. Paul is holding fast to the ideal, but he is dealing at the same time with realities.

"Do not divorce."

"But if you do" divorce, remain unmarried or be reconciled. That second statement sounds just as blunt and final as the first! So the question we must ask is this: *Is* it final? Is there no exception to the "remain unmarried" instruction? Is there a terminal point for the waiting, or must one wait forever, no matter what the ex-spouse may do?

Believers and unbelievers

One of the realities in Corinth had to do with the strongly pagan culture in which the Church sprang up. Corinth was a center of immorality in Paul's day. "To Corinthianize" was slang for engaging in all sorts of sexual excesses. When a person in Corinth turned from paganism to Christ, his marriage was very likely to be affected. A completely different moral orientation was the result.

Paul is careful to instruct husbands and wives that they are not to initiate divorces against their pagan spouses. Even though God has said, "Do not be mismated with unbelievers" (2 Cor. 6:14, RSV), he does not want the Christians to initiate divorce. Yet many Christians were troubled by the fact that their pagan spouses had divorced *them!*

These new Christians had been taught the biblical ideal. Marriage is a permanent, lifelong relationship. Jesus' own teaching is, "Do not divorce." Had they sinned because their pagan spouses chose to divorce them? Were they guilty? Should they be cast out of the Christian community?

Here Paul says a surprising thing. "If the unbelieving

partner desires to separate, let it be so; in such a case the brother or sister is not bound. For God has called us to peace. Wife, how do you know whether you will save your husband? Husband, how do you know whether you will save your wife?" (1 Cor. 7:15–16, RSV).

This is a surprising argument.

Paul has just stated the "remain unmarried" principle. Now he seems to change the rules. Instead of treating this precept as a final statement, Paul suggests that in the case of a believer deserted by an unbeliever, there is no bond. The circumstances are such that the believing man or woman is free. The reason Paul gives? "You can't know whether your ex-husband or ex-wife will be converted!"

Without conversion there is no basis to expect reconciliation. For reconciliation demands a "greatness" lifestyle which is fully possible only to those who have received God's forgiveness.

"But Paul! Shouldn't the believer wait to see if perhaps God will work? Shouldn't the prescription to remain unmarried be applied as long as the least *possibility* of reconciliation exists?"

And again Paul's answer comes. "God has called us to peace." The believer is "not bound" in these circumstances. For him or her the divorce has become a doorway to a freedom that, as in Old Testament times, implies the right of remarriage.

Adultery

At this point we must return to Jesus' description of remarriage as adultery. Is this true of *all* cases of remarriage? Or is a remarriage such as the one Paul deals with in the case above free of that stigma?

Jesus' own statement, recorded in Matthew 19:9, suggests that there are exceptions. He says that in the case of "marital infidelity" remarriage is not even technical adultery. Often in Jesus' day, as in our own, divorce was *for the purpose of* marrying another partner. Certainly if lusting in one's heart for another involves adultery (Matt. 5:28), there can be no doubt that to desert a spouse to marry another is adulterous behavior. Yet statement of the "marital infidelity" exception just as clearly indicates that not every remarriage involves adultery. A marriage shattered by the hardness of one partner's heart may fully release one for remarriage.

The issue of legitimate remarriage is confused by a misunderstanding of the nature of the adultery which is involved. Some have taught that to remarry is to enter an *adulterous relationship.* By this interpretation, to live with a second husband or second wife is to *live in a state of sin.*

This is a very unlikely interpretation. In the Old Testament, adultery was not only condemned, it was to be dealt with by stoning the adulterous pair. Yet in the Old Testament remarriage was a valid social institution. If an adulterous *state* were involved, God surely would have dealt with the sin more severely. He would at least have commanded the separation of couples who had entered into second marriages.

But there is no hint of such teaching in the Old Testament. There is no hint of such teaching in the New. Jesus is clear about the ideal and clear about the sin. But in no place does he prescribe separation for those who have remarried. Even when a second marriage does involve adultery, we must conclude that the adultery relates not to the marriage as a whole, but only to the act by which the second marriage is initiated. The physical consummation of the new union may technically and in reality be an adulterous act. In such a case, it must be acknowledged as sin, and dealt with as sin. It must be brought to the Lord in confession, expecting him to keep his promise to forgive and cleanse. But at the same time the second union *is* initiated. A new and valid marriage relationship has been established. Within the framework of that new marriage, sexual relations once again take on the holy and undefiled character that God gave them within marriage.

At this point, then, I've suggested that even when a remarriage does involve adultery, the adultery relates to the initiating *act* and not to the *state* (the marriage relationship as a whole). In this case, forgiveness is required—and available. But I have also suggested that in some cases remarriage does *not* involve adultery, that God can in fact lead believers into second marriages which are totally free of that stigma.

We see a parallel in the commandment, "You shall not kill." Taking another human life is wrong. And the murderer is to be punished. Yet the Law makes provision for one who kills another accidentally. And in war, killing is legitimate. Certainly, taking another human life under any circumstance falls short of God's ideal of the way in which people are to live together. Yet because of the impact of sin on society, situations do arise in which taking life is legitimate and free from the stigma of murder.

Should we be surprised then that in some situations remarriage, which admittedly can involve adultery, may not involve adultery at all? When Jesus states the "marital unfaithfulness" exception, he opens the door to exploration of Scripture to see if other exceptions exist as well!

Other exceptions?

If the final-sounding statement, "She must remain unmarried or be reconciled to her husband," is in fact a principle with one exception, might there be more exceptions? Following the thought of Paul, that where there is no reasonable expectation of reconciliation the Christian is not to be bound, we might suggest the following.

• Don's wife has remarried. Certainly we can see him as unbound. There is no possibility of reconciliation in Don's case.

• Diana is a new Christian, and her husband is not a believer. Following Paul's guidelines about such marriages, there is no reason why she should see herself as bound. She, too, is free to remarry.

• Marilyn's husband left her and established a homosexual relationship with another man. In spite of all her efforts, he remained unmoved. There seems no basis to expect a change of heart for him either. It seems that Marilyn also should open her life to the possibility that remarriage is in God's plan for her.

All of these people have been brutalized by sin. Sin in themselves, and sin in others. They each bear their own responsibility for the relationship which has been broken. Each one is, as an active or a passive participant, involved in the tragic sin of divorce. Each may at some future time become partners with another in remarriage.

And if they do?

How will we in the Christian community relate to them? Will we condemn or ostracize them? Will we be afraid to accept them and treat them with grace, for fear that acceptance would encourage others to divorce and remarry as well?

Or will we sympathize with them in their suffering and welcome them among us with forgiveness? You see, none of the persons I've written about *wanted* a divorce. Each wanted the ideal! Each honestly struggled in his or her marriage to work toward the ideal. In each case, however, the effects of sin destroyed their hopes and ravaged them. In each case sin, building its beachhead in the personality of the partner, caused

Remarriage

a situation that could be dealt with only through divorce.

If they do seek remarriage, not one of those I've written about will be moved by what we could call an "unholy passion." No one will consider remarrying because of a desire for illicit sex. Each one will act only when driven by deep personal need, and be moved by an honest, true love for another human being to whom each is willing to commit his or her total life. Each will act only as he or she feels led by God! Each one's remarriage, if it takes place, will be "for life." The goal of that new marriage will be to seek, together, the experience of God's ideal.

Why laws fail

In our examination of Scripture in this chapter we've come across statements couched in terms of commands that sound both final and exceptionless. And then, in the very passage where these statements are made, we find exceptions stated!

How can we explain this?

We can explain it by realizing that God seldom speaks to us in exceptionless laws. God knows only too well the impact of sin on our human condition. He shares with us the ideal, the best. He says boldly, "This is my will!" But when achievement of that will is beyond us, he meets us with forgiveness and with grace.

Grace says that when life has gone wrong, God understands. He will act to forgive and to restore.

It's best to take God's expressions of his will as guidelines rather than exceptionless demands, as principles or statements of ideals rather than as rules we dare not break. Each of us will normally follow such guidelines . . . and in following, will find a grace from God that lifts us beyond our own potentials. When we live this way, dependent on God, eager to respond, willing to humble ourselves and obey the voice of God, we find healing in every relationship. And in marriage as well.

But God, who wants the best for us, can also face the *unusual* case. He can handle the situation in which his child honestly tries but for some reason cannot achieve. It is in the unusual case that grace and mercy step forward. It is in the unusual situation that divorce, and remarriage, are given legitimate standing by God.

God has not drawn back from his ideal.

But God *has* drawn close to us.

He has stooped to touch us in the dust where we lie broken by our disappointment and our lost hope. He has stooped to tell us, "Acknowledge your failure. But acknowledge too my capacity to forgive and to rebuild your life."

He has stooped to tell us that he will, in grace, affirm remarriage as a legitimate act.

8

Shall "I Do" It?

"Well, will your dad marry us then?" Andrea waited anxiously for her cousin's answer.

"I . . . I just don't know," Kim told her. "I'll ask him."

Andrea had put everyone in such an uncomfortable position. The divorce was bad enough. Andrea had felt *so* guilty, you just had to be sorry for her. Of course, Andrea felt guilty every time she missed a Sunday evening service!

The family had disapproved of the divorce, of course. And her church friends roundly condemned it. Walter had been immature, yes. And hard to live with. But he hadn't been an adulterer. So there were no real legitimate grounds for the divorce.

Still, Walt had been hard to live with. And he'd kept on deserting Andrea . . . leaving her for a week or month and telling her he wanted to end their marriage. Then he'd come back, say he'd changed his mind, and expect everything to be the way it was before.

Finally the strain of that and the new baby had driven Andrea to the edge of nervous exhaustion. She simply couldn't stand the uncertainty any more. So she filed for a divorce. Then, keeping to his pattern, Walt came back again. When he found out about the divorce action, he was distraught. Now that he was about to lose what he'd never really wanted, he wanted it desperately! Walt had even cried, begging Andrea to take him back. He'd called Kim and all the other relatives, telling them how changed he'd be, and begging them to get Andrea to change her mind.

Then the divorce was final, and only a month later Andrea had begun dating Jon. It was a whirlwind romance. That first month Jon had proposed. And now, just three months after her divorce, Andrea was determined to remarry. Strikingly, Walt had found someone else too.

Both of these Christian young people, in spite of the overwhelming disapproval of their churches and relatives, were ready to rush into a marriage to replace the one that had so tragically failed.

Another option

So far in this book I have suggested that the Christian community recognize remarriage as a valid option for believers, as a legitimate act. But let's also be clear about the fact that it is not the sole option. There is another option that may well be the better choice for many. Paul describes this option:

> Are you bound to a wife? Do not seek to be free. Are you free from a wife? Do not seek marriage. But if you marry, you do not sin, and if a girl marries she does not sin. Yet those who marry will have worldly troubles, and I would spare you that. I mean, brethren, the appointed time has grown very short. . . .

Remarriage

I want you to be free from anxieties. The unmarried man is anxious about the affairs of the Lord, how to please the Lord; but the married man is anxious about worldly affairs, how to please his wife, and his interests are divided. And the unmarried woman or girl is anxious about the affairs of the Lord, how to be holy in body and spirit; but the married woman is anxious about worldly affairs, how to please her husband.—1 Corinthians 7:27–29, 32–34, RSV

These words from the Apostle may seem cold. They are not meant to be. They are meant to help us deal with the realities of life and to evaluate our own motives and goals. As Paul goes on to point out, "I say this for your own benefit, not to lay any restraint upon you" (v. 35, RSV). Paul knows, as we all do, that to live as a married person or to live as an unmarried person is a matter of gift.

So he encourages us to carefully consider the option of remaining unmarried.

Divorce even today may be a doorway to remarriage. But remarriage is not the kind of choice anyone ought to make unthinkingly.

Marriage involves each of us in a life of personal compromises. It demands a selflessness that includes at times surrender of even our spiritual priorities to give spouse and family the priority they require.

Bill, a single guy, is committed to giving to many different ministries. He lives simply—some would say cheaply—and while his income is significantly large, he contributes most of it to Christian work. Bill has thought about marriage. But if he marries there will be a dramatic impact on his giving pattern. There'll be a house to buy, more clothing and food to buy, medical and dental bills as the kids grow up. A bigger car to carry them. Insurance. All these things are right and good, and it would be important for Bill to show love to his wife in financial ways, even as he now employs his money to show love to the Lord. But he's thought about the changes marriage would make in his priorities. And he's uncertain.

Jana works with a "para church" ministry. And she uses her music gifts singing in many different situations. Marriage for Jana would mean a change in her lifestyle. Could she keep up her involvements and still love a husband? The priorities would have to conflict: the lifestyle change would be a dramatic one. Like any normal person, Jana's thought of marriage. But is marriage right for her? Or is she finding her fulfillment and her call in the ministries in which she's proven so effective?

This is the kind of question Paul encourages us to ask. If we've never been married, it's the kind of question that should be asked before taking that step into the married life. And if we have married and divorced, it is the kind of question we should be even more concerned about than ever. Before we remarry, we need to ask ourselves and God, "Is this my calling?" And we need to be *sure* before we rush through the open doorway of divorce and launch another marriage in haste.

Andrea has never really considered the option of the single life. She's been swept, in two brief months, into the romantic trap of our day that insists on seeing marriage as an idealized state in which our fulfillment can be found. Andrea has given marriage one try, and discovered that neither she nor the man she chose had the maturity and commitment necessary for the greatness lifestyle that marriage demands. Now she's about to marry a man she hardly knows at all in the naïve expectation that this time it will be "different"!

It won't.

Andrea and her intended have shown an immaturity in their rush toward remarriage that tells us unquestionably that neither one is ready to deal with the reality of that relationship.

Why remarry?

God has given us several guidelines that help us think wisely about marriage and remarriage. Let's say first of all that one of the valid reasons for marriage is sexual need. "They should marry," Paul advises, "for it is better to marry than to be aflame with passion" (1 Cor. 7:9, RSV). Marriage is the context in which God has made gracious provision for the satisfaction of sexual needs, and in the relationship of marriage he acts to lift sex beyond the "animal need" level. For married couples sex can become a symbol and expression of complete openness with each other. It can become for them what it is intended by God's design to be: participation through the symbol in the reality of our union with Jesus Christ himself as his bride, the Church.

Another motive for marriage or remarriage is found in the Creation account: "The two shall become one." Our personal enrichment, our growth together in the relationship of marriage into something neither one of us could be alone, is a central goal.

In 1 Thessalonians 4:4–5 we are warned against marrying "in lustful passion as the heathen do" (TLB). Paul is not talking here primarily of sex. The Greek word for "passion" speaks of all strong human drives and desires. To "marry in passion" in this passage means to marry with the motive of having our spouse serve to meet our personal needs.

Some marry because of a need to be dependent. In such a marriage the adult tries to relate as a child to his or her spouse; the mate is simply a replacement for mom or dad. Others marry because of a drive for dominance. They need someone they can master, who will relate to them as a slave. All too often the male insistence on being "head of the house" is not an expression of the biblical meaning of headship, but is instead an expression of an immature need to have someone to dominate.

When Linda married Luke her motive was not love, but simply that he, a "spiritual man," might make her a more spiritual person. The desire was commendable. But the motive was an inadequate one as the basis for a marriage relationship.

We can think of so many different motives people have for marriage which are in the realm of passions. A need for security. A desire to be socially prominent. A desire for wealth. Pride in the looks of the one we choose as a partner.

When dating and moving toward marriage, we usually carefully avoid an honest examination of our motives. We idealize our potential mate and what marriage to them will be like. Because of our romantic idealizations, we fail to begin our marriages with the awareness that life with any other human being will bring pain as well as joy, hurt as well as help. We are unrealistic about the demands for a gracious and greatness lifestyle that marriage will place on us. And when our idealizations shatter under the hammer blows of the reality of life in this heart-hardened universe, we are crushed. Too many of us turn blindly to divorce as the answer. And too many of us then rush into remarriages based on the same empty and foolish notions that caused the ruin of our first relationships.

Andrea's rush toward hasty remarriage shows how little she has learned from the first tragedy. God's gracious provision for divorce and remarriage is being *misused* in her case. God's intention in providing for legitimate remarriage was to meet the needs of the unusual case . . . the case like that of Don or Marilyn where, in spite of mature and honest effort to live

Remarriage

by God's ideal, the marriage became a casualty in the war of sin against humanity.

Can Andrea remarry? Yes. Where God gives us freedom, any freedom, there is the potential for that freedom to be misused. And when we misuse freedom there is still forgiveness available. God can even redeem the second marriage Andrea seems intent on rushing into. But God's permission of divorce and remarriage is not *intended* to make our foolishness easier, or to make marriage a thing we lightly enter into.

But, why remarry?

We still haven't answered that question. I've suggested that one valid motive is to meet sexual needs in the context God has provided for that purpose. But there is far more to marriage than this.

Basically, the answer is found in *servanthood.*

In Matthew 20, toward the end of the teaching sequence and events that outline greatness for us, Jesus talks about rule and authority. He points out that the secular ruler "lords it over" others, and from that position relies on "authority" to get them to accomplish his will. The secular approach always tends to do this. To *use* others and to bend them to our purposes.

But Jesus went on to say, "Not so among you." The Christian approach is very different. We are to live "among" our brothers and sisters as one of them, and in that relationship alongside them we are to *serve.* Jesus put it this way: "Whoever would be great among you must be your servant, and whoever would be first among you must be your slave; even as the Son of man came not to be served but to serve, and to give his life as a ransom for many" (Matt. 20:26–28, RSV).

The Christian who walks Jesus' path toward greatness has a whole new set of motives. He or she desires to serve: not to use others, but to give his or her life for the other's benefit. This is the key to a meaningful and fulfilling marriage as well. Do I love the person with whom I choose to link my life? Am I willing, because I truly care, to serve my spouse? Will I spend my life for his or her sake?

When we approach marriage from the servanthood point of view, there is a real and dramatic change. Because we honestly seek each other's highest good, we have a basis for total trust. Because we honestly care about the other's needs and the other's growth, we can work through disagreements without having to fight for our "rights." Because we find our joy in enriching the other person and in sensing God's transforming work in his or her life, we find true fulfillment. And, because our spouse has the same deep desire to serve and enrich us, we two are on our way to becoming one.

The final touch

The sequence in these three chapters of Matthew's Gospel ends with this beautiful story (20:29–34). Jesus and his disciples are leaving Jericho on the way to Jerusalem, where Jesus knows he will face crucifixion. Along the way the crowds have gathered to watch this wonder-worker pass. And there, in the background, we can just make out two blind men.

"What's happening?" they call out.

Someone in the crowd mumbles, "Jesus of Nazareth. He's passing by this way."

Excited at the news, the blind men begin to cry his name. "Lord, Son of David, have mercy on us!" (20:30).

The people near them are irritated. "Hush up," they scold. They want to hear if Jesus should say anything as he passes by. But the two blind men cry out all the louder. Now you can hear the angry murmuring of the people around them. Who are these shouters, anyway? Nothing but a couple of blind beggars. More of the worthless scum of the poor that infest the land.

But Jesus stopped.

Jesus called to them.

In spite of the terrible prospect of his own coming death, in spite of the inner pressures and anguish he was experiencing just then, Jesus stopped and called them. And this is what he said (v. 32):

"What do you want me to do for you?"

This is the foundation on which we must build our marriages . . . and our remarriages. Are we ready to step into a relationship in which we will love as Jesus loved, and serve as Jesus served? Are we ready to marry, not to meet our own needs, but because love has called us to a ministry of commitment to a husband or wife to whom we will speak our Lord's own servant words, "What do you want me to do for you?"

9

Mercy—
and Grace to Help

Christians, and the Church, must always live in tension. It is the tension between God's call to the ideal and the pull of sin which drags down toward the real.

Many Christians cannot live with this kind of tension. So they attempt to deny it or to block themselves off from it. Some cry out to God for power, certain that if only today we had the same commitment as those in the early Church, all our problems could be resolved, and we would know some form of perfection here. Others turn to legalism to build barriers against the real. If we can only erect some unbreakable law, then "they" will be outside, and "we" will be safe within.

But none of these approaches is the one God has chosen. God has chosen a delicate balance between mercy and grace that he might meet us *in* our tension.

Tension between real and ideal can never be avoided. Such tension is something we must learn to live with and meet in God's way. John says of Jesus, "And the Word became flesh and dwelt among us, full of grace and truth; we have beheld his glory, glory as of the only Son from the Father" (John 1:14, RSV). We need to learn Jesus' glorious way, the way of grace and truth.

An easy out?

I know that some will insist on seeing what I have written in this book as promoting divorce and remarriage. They will see it as an easy way out for weak people, a license to choose a course they might not otherwise pick.

I am not encouraging an easy way out. I am not promoting divorce. I am not counseling remarriage. What I am trying to do is deal with this most difficult and hurting subject in a perspective that is shaped by basic theology. I am trying to interpret the words of the passages that deal with divorce and remarriage in light provided by the whole of God's revelation.

If we do come from such a theological perspective, it is difficult to justify a "law" interpretation of what Jesus or the Apostle Paul says.

Law came through Moses.

Grace came through Jesus.

"Sin will have no dominion over you," Paul says, and explains the new freedom in these words: "you are not under law but under grace" (Rom. 6:14, RSV). How strange it would be if these two proponents of grace in every other situation were to actually establish a more difficult law in the one instance of marriage!

If we seek an instance of a New Testament command, we would turn more quickly to John 13 than to Matthew 19. In John 13:34, Jesus says, "A new commandment I give to you, that you love one another; even as I have loved you, that you also love one another" (RSV). And what about the command that love mark our relationships within the Church? This theme is constantly repeated in every Epistle. And the Epistles also recount failures to live up to that ideal!

The Corinthian church split over leaders, over doctrines, over spiritual gifts. Paul had to call them, in the most blunt language, "unspiritual." In Philippi two leading women, Euodia and Syntyche, fell into a bitter feud. Paul pleaded with them to "agree in the Lord" (Phil. 4:2, RSV). Paul himself broke with his closest brother, Barnabas, over whether or not John Mark should accompany them on a second missionary venture.

These men and women had an ideal set before them. It was an ideal couched in the form of a command. And even such spiritual giants as Paul and Barnabas fell short. The reality of their lives failed to match the ideal to which they, and the whole Church, were committed.

How does God deal with such failures? In terms of the persons involved, by counseling the way of greatness. "Be kind to one another, tenderhearted, forgiving one another, as God in Christ forgave you" (Eph. 4:32, RSV). When in the tension between real and ideal we fall, a Divine kind of compassion and forgiveness is to operate in our fellowships.

We are not to erect more rigid rules to try to control behavior. We are to trust our brother and sister to want to respond to God, and we are to help them respond by giving support and by extending forgiveness. We are to take the mantle of grace and mercy worn so comfortably by Jesus and to wrap that mantle around ourselves and our brothers.

It's much harder for us to deal with tensions between real and ideal than to deny them—or to write off our fellows who have failed. But any retreat to law is in some sense a denial of grace.

Remarriage

Grace to help

As Christians we are invited to come to the throne of grace to receive "grace to help in time of need" (Heb. 4:16, RSV). This is our one and secure hope for achievement of God's ideals.

In each of us there is still a tendency toward sin. There is still a weakness that makes it impossible for us to achieve in our own strength. Jesus said it well: "apart from me you can do nothing" (John 15:5, RSV). But Jesus has acted to counter our weaknesses. In the same discourse, recorded in John 14–16, Jesus speaks of the Person of the Holy Spirit, who comes alongside us to support and enable. Because God the Holy Spirit is present in us, we can be lifted by his action beyond our own potential. We can make godly choices, and we can live out those choices in a redeeming way.

For the married, this tells us that the way to greatness is not closed. No matter how deep the hurt. No matter how painful the past. God's action in our lives can show us the way to forgiveness and reconciliation.

Our emphasis in counseling married couples must always be placed on the availability of the power of God to redeem the relationship. If the couple will only come boldly to the throne of God's grace, they will find grace to help.

But what if one or both members of that couple refuse to come? What if they turn away from the offered resources? Then they shut themselves off from the helping power of God, and in every likelihood doom their marriage to a divorce.

It is at this point that we need to come to them with a message not of law but of mercy. For this is another fact about the throne of grace. We find mercy there as well as help. Grace upholds us as we struggle with the real/ideal tension. Mercy meets us after we have fallen. Both are needed. Both are vital. Because this world is marred by hardness of heart, both will always be required. We will never be completely free until the day of our final redemption when all is made beautiful and new.

But what then does it mean when the writer says "come boldly"? It means simply this: We can come to God with the *total assurance* that however great our need for either mercy or helping grace, God will richly provide it. God will never hold back from children whose weaknesses Jesus so fully understands.

What right then do we have to erect law—when God himself has abandoned a law approach to life— to block the divorced and remarried from assured approach to grace?

Truth

The word *truth* in Scripture is a fascinating one. Both the Greek and Hebrew words give us a sense of "in full correspondence with reality." A thing is "true" not simply because God says it, but also because what he says is an accurate expression of the way things actually are. Grace and truth came together in Jesus. With truth he enables us to penetrate to the realities of our situation and by grace he enables us to deal with reality in a healthy, godly way.

When Jesus spoke of divorce and remarriage to the Pharisees, he was not discussing Law nor setting up higher law. He was revealing truth. He was helping them see the real issues involved in divorce and remarriage, so they would not deal with this vital subject so lightly. They had asked, "Is it lawful to divorce one's wife for *any cause?*" How far can we go in permitting divorce? was their concern. But Jesus' concern was for the damage to the persons involved. Jesus' concern was for the hurt that sin always induces in our lives. So Jesus spoke the truth, and in speaking the truth attempted to help the Pharisees deal with the reality of human suffering rather than the legalities behind which they hid. Jesus asked them to enter the real world of hurting men and women, and stop retreating to Law as a barrier against that pain.

There is no evidence the Pharisees understood Jesus at all. If they had faced the reality of sin they might even have been willing to turn away from legalism and seek some remedy in grace. But their hearts too were hard. They loved sacrifice . . . the rituals of their religion. But they were unconcerned about mercy . . . the quality that God was concerned about more than all.

I believe it's time that we who are the followers of Jesus Christ reject the word games Pharisees liked to play, and face with Jesus truth, mercy, and grace.

Truth enables us to deal with the ideal and the real. We can affirm the ideal and still admit the fact of failure to achieve it.

Grace enables us to hold out hope to the married and the unmarried. Grace frees us to affirm an enabling power of God that, as husband and wife rely on him, can redeem a marriage even though it has been racked with pain.

Mercy enables us to deal, as God did, with those who somehow fail to grasp firmly enough the grace provided. Mercy enables us to accept the person who has suffered through the agony of divorce, and may now be moving toward remarriage.

Truth, grace, and mercy all testify to God's compassionate motives in permitting, through the Old Testament age and even today, remarriage as his direct and guided will for some of his children.

PART II

The Scriptures

Methodology

In this part of the book I want simply to examine those passages in the Gospels and Epistles which deal with divorce and remarriage. It's not my purpose in this study to line up authorities on one side or the other of the issue. If you want such a study, I recommend InterVarsity Press's 1990 book, *Four Views on Divorce and Remarriage*.

What I want to do here is to explore directly what the Bible says, with particular attention to three critical issues. The three are *context*, *truth*, and *grace*.

By context I mean primarily the historical context in which Jesus spoke, and in which the apostle Paul wrote. Before we can grasp the point that is made in the biblical passages we'll look at, we need to understand how the people of the first century, in Israel and in the wider gentile world, viewed divorce and remarriage. When we understand their perspective, we will be able to see often striking contrasts in the view that Jesus, in particular, expresses.

Remarriage

By truth I mean something I discussed in chapter 9. In both testaments the concept of "truth" finds its roots in "correspondence with reality." Ephesians describes lost humanity as condemned to "drift along on this world's ideas of living," so that we are trapped in a world of "illusion" (Eph. 2:1–5). God's Word comes to us as a bright light, exposing our errors, and revealing the true nature of all things. In the light shed by Scripture we discover the errors in man's distorted values and viewpoint. In Scripture we learn God's perspective on life situations. When we adopt that perspective, we are guided to right and godly choices.

It is here that context and truth relate so intimately. As we explore the historical context, we see how first century society perceived the issue of divorce and remarriage. Then, in the light shed by Christ and the apostle Paul, we see the reality: we see how God views these issues that are so painful and so real to so many of us today. So it is vitally important to carefully trace the thought of each passage dealing with divorce and remarriage. Only by looking at the flow of the passage in which verses on divorce and remarriage are found can we learn the truth, can we see this issue as God sees it, and accurately sense his leading in our own lives.

By grace I mean far more than the "unmerited favor of God." Grace is the essence of God's saving act in Jesus Christ, flowing freely from his sacrifical death. Grace is the basis for relationship between God and man. With sin's penalty paid, God is free to relate to us in love and acceptance, rather than on the basis of how poorly or how well our actions conform to his standards. The grace that brings us salvation continues to operate after we are saved. We will, at times, fall. But God's forgiveness is endless, and his power to cleanse and transform us is without limit. No mistake we make is so terrible that the redemptive power of grace cannot remold it, and us. No error is so appalling God is unable to transform its evil into good, and its pain into joy. Grace means that God is committed to work with us throughout our lives here on earth. Grace means that while God does not condone sin, neither does he condemn the sinner. And the principle of grace that shines so brightly in Jesus Christ *must be applied as we study the question of divorce and marriage.*

John 1:17 says it. "For the law was given through Moses; grace and truth came through Jesus Christ."

Those who retreat to legalistic "you cannot" rulings in their treatment of divorce and remarriage are not even in the company of Moses, who permitted divorce. They are surely not in the company of Jesus, who came not to burden a weak humanity with even stricter law, but to bring us a unique message of grace and truth. And the truth, as we shall see, is that God is gracious to those who fail in marriage. The truth is that God does give those who ache for companionship and love another chance.

10

Matthew 5:31, 32

"It has been said, 'Anyone who divorces his wife must give her a certificate of divorce.' But I tell you that anyone who divorces his wife, except for marital unfaithfulness, causes her to commit adultery, and anyone who marries a woman so divorced commits adultery."

Context. In Deuteronomy 24 Moses speaks of a "certificate of divorce" which a husband would write out and give to his wife in order to divorce her. That passage speaks of her becoming "displeasing" because he finds "something indecent about her." The Hebrew phrase, *'erwat dabar,* was interpreted in two ways in Jesus' day. Rabbi Shammai and his followers considered the two words a single phrase, meaning "an unchaste way." But Rabbi Hillel separated the two words, and held that either unchastity (*'erwat*) or any "way" (*dabar:* a habit, practice, characteristic, i.e., *anything* displeasing) was a valid ground for divorce. Study of first century marriage contracts, as well as the writings of the first century Jewish historian Josephus and the Jewish philosopher Philo, indicate that in Christ's day the school of Hillel dominated. Divorce depended pretty much on the caprice of the husband. As custom required a husband to repay the wife's dowry [*ketubah*] if he divorced her for any reason other than adultery, divorce was not as common as the generally accepted view of the husband's right to shed his wife for any cause might imply.

It is important to note that the Greek word translated "marital unfaithfulness" in Mt. 5:31, 32, *porneia*, undoubtedly reflects the Hebrew phrase *'erwat dabar*. But our problem is that, just as the meaning of the Hebrew phrase was much debated in first century Judaism, the meaning of *porneia* in this context is also uncertain. The *New International Dictionary of New Testament Theology* (Colin Brown, ed; vol. 1, p. 147) states that in later Jewish rabbinic teaching *porneia* was understood to include "not only prostitution and any kind of extra-marital sexual intercourse, but also all marriages between relatives forbidden by rabbinical law. Incest and all kinds of unnatural sexual intercourse were viewed as fornication (*porneia*)."

What we see from context, then, is that when Jesus spoke the words recorded in Matthew 5:31, 32 there was a debate over the grounds on which a man might divorce his wife. The meaning of a key phrase in Deuteronomy 24 was unclear, and society as a whole had adopted the rather liberal view of Rabbi Hillel rather than the more strict view of Rabbi Shammai. The fact that the issue of divorce was raised by the Pharisees (see Matt. 19) indicates the question was still hotly debated, and that the focus of the debate was the conditions under which a certificate of divorce might lawfully be written out by the husband.

But why were the rabbis so concerned over the obscure language? Because all Israel understood that God through Moses had given his covenant people a law. And all Israel was convinced that it was their duty and privilege to keep God's commandments. By the first century most of the Jewish people were sure that their hope of salvation depended on keeping the law as faithfully as possible. A person who kept the law was a righteous person, and would surely enter into the kingdom of God. Thus *every* law was important, and every legal question was as hotly debated as the law of divorce and remarriage.

In fact, as we turn to Matthew 5, we discover that the truth Jesus seeks to reveal has to do not with divorce as such, but with the more basic issue of his listeners' attitude toward law!

Truth. When we study the passage, we're surprised to see that Jesus is not dealing with the question of divorce and remarriage as such. True, Jesus makes a pronouncement about divorce and adultery. And he does note a situation in which remarriage after divorce does *not* involve adultery. But he mentions divorce as an illustration in a string of illustrations, which together are intended to reveal a stunning truth. And that stunning truth gives us perspective on the meaning of Matthew 5:31, 32 for us.

We find that truth by tracing the argument of a key section within the Sermon on the Mount. The passage begins with a statement by Jesus about law. He has been accused by his enemies of rejecting the Law and the Prophets in his teaching. Now Jesus says, "Think not that I have come to abolish the law and the prophets; I have come not to abolish them but to fulfill them" (Matt. 5:17, RSV).

There has been much debate about the meaning of the word *fulfil*. However, the people of Jesus' day understood exactly what he was saying. He was promising to do what every rabbi gave his life to do. To fulfill the Law meant to explain its meaning in a complete and accurate way. To fulfill the Law meant to penetrate to the heart of *the* Divine revelation, to expose the beauty of it for all to see, that the life of the believer might be shaped toward its glory. Jesus' promise to "fulfil the law" was a promise to expose the reality underlying the words of Scripture.

For those who saw Law as a way either to spiritual greatness or to establish one's relationship with God, Jesus had a warning. Law is firmly established. Anyone who approaches God by the avenue of Law must practice it all. For them to practice a "fulfilled" Law demands an unimaginable righteousness. "Unless your righteousness exceeds that of the Scribes and Pharisees, you will never enter the kingdom of heaven" (Matt. 5:20, RSV).

At this point Jesus introduces a series of "you have heard that it was said" sayings. In each Jesus first quotes the Mosaic Code. He then penetrates to the *ideal* which is both expressed and hidden in Law. A look at three of them helps put Jesus' statement on divorce and remarriage in appropriate context.

Murder. "You have heard that it was said to the people long ago, 'Do not murder, and anyone who murders will be subject to judgment.' But I tell you that anyone who is angry with his brother will be subject to judgment" (Matt. 5:21–22).

Adultery. "You have heard that it was said 'Do not commit adultery.' But I tell you that anyone who looks at a woman lustfully has already committed adultery with her in his heart." (5:27–28).

Divorce. And, in the immediate context, "It has been

Remarriage

said, 'Anyone who divorces his wife must give her a certificate of divorce.' But I tell you that anyone who divorces his wife, except for marital unfaithfulness, causes her to commit adultery, and anyone who marries a woman so divorced commits adultery" (5:31–32).

We immediately notice a striking thing about the first two of this triad. Each states a law which deals with an *action* and then immediately moves beyond behavior to deal with *motives.* In the cases of both murder and adultery, Jesus condemns the inner anger and lust that are the wellsprings of the behavior. What is striking about this is that while Law can deal with acts of sin, no legislation can deal with one's hidden motives and desires.

But in a revelation of reality this teaching is important. It was too easy for a man living under Law not to act out his sinfulness and to make the mistake of thinking himself righteous before God! This was one of the errors of the Pharisees. They struggled to, and in the main did, keep the letter of Law. But they violated the spirit of the Law in their hearts. This is the reality Jesus forced his listeners to face. If Law, and the root of Law in the holy character of God, are truly understood, then no one can claim righteousness.

Jesus' statements about murder and adultery then were never meant to be incorporated into the social and legal code of Israel. He never intended that a person who shouted out anger against his brother be brought to trial for murder. He never intended that a person who entertains lustful thoughts should be stoned to death for mental adultery.

When the true meaning of Law, the fulfilled meaning, was grasped by Israel, they would see how futile it is to seek standing with God by their acts of righteousness.

What are the implications when we find Jesus' statement about divorce in this context, and in the same form as the statements about murder and adultery? For one thing, if the first two are not intended as a basis for social legislation, but instead as an expression of the reality revealed and hidden in Law, then it seems unreasonable to argue that the third statement *is* intended as a basis of new legislation. If we persist in seeing Jesus' statement here as the statement of a new law, then we will find no support for our view in sound hermeneutics.

Truth. Now, note the implications of the truth Jesus has taken such pains to drive home.

Jesus' statement about divorce and remarriage is found in a series of six "you have heard" sayings. Each of these, like Jesus' saying about murder and the adulterous look, are intended to show that while the rulings of the law deal with behavior, God is concerned about the heart. A person can keep every law, and still lack the righteousness required to enter the Kingdom of Heaven.

As we look at the illustrations, it's clear that Jesus is *not* introducing "higher law." We make laws against murder, but hardly against anger. We make laws against adultery, but who could enforce a law against lustful thoughts? In fact, *not one* of Jesus' other five illustrations here is intended as the basis for social legislation! How utterly strange, then, that some believers today insist on seeing Matthew 5:31, 32 as Christ's definition of a "higher law" against divorce and remarriage that is binding on modern Christians!

The truth that Jesus sought to reveal to his Jewish brothers and sisters is, simply, that law isn't everything. God, who gave the law, is concerned with our hearts and not just our behavior. If we are truly to be righteous, our hearts as well as our actions must be right.

Remarriage

In this teaching Jesus challenged his people's view of God's law, and created a terrible problem. If God judges our hearts, who can possibly stand before him? Jesus then went on to live, and to die, to provide the answer.

No one can stand before God. Every human being who has ever lived has fallen short. And so God, in love, became a man to die for our shortcomings. He offers us salvation as a gift of grace. And he calls on us to live transformed lives, strengthened by his grace.

If we fall, as we all too often will, we can come freely to him for forgiveness. And in him we can also find the grace we need to try again and to succeed.

Grace. The teaching of Jesus in this passage simply can not lay a heavier burden on modern Christians whose marriages have failed than Mosaic Law laid on the Jews. In fact, Jesus' teaching gives us a new perspective on divorce and remarriage. It reminds us that a legalistic approach to the issues of life is wrong. God is fully aware of all our sins and failings. And he has chosen to relate to us in grace, pouring out forgiveness. Ultimately, as we walk with the Lord, that same grace will transform us. God will cleanse us of the anger that causes us to strike out at others and leads many to murder. God will purify us so we value others as persons rather than look at them merely as sex objects. And God will purge us of our unwillingness to forgive and to accept forgiveness, traits that ruin so many marriages.

Who can doubt that the God who forgives sin also extends us the freedom, when the pain of divorce finally heals, to try again?

11

Matthew 19:3–12

Context. The context of the Pharisees' questions was outlined at the beginning of chapter 10. The Pharisees here ask Jesus which school of thought on divorce he holds to: that of Shammai, or that of Hillel?

But before we can go on to see the Truth Jesus reveals here, we need to understand one more thing about first century Jewish culture.

When the Jerusalem Temple was destroyed in 587 B.C. and the Jews were deported to Babylon, the people began to focus on the study of Scripture. Even after returning to the land and rebuilding the temple, weekly gatherings were held in village synagogues to study the Old Testament laws. While everyone was expected to study the Old Testament, some men devoted their lives to this exercise. Gradually a religious elite developed: "scribes" who were recognized experts in biblical law. These scribes might be members of the priestly class (the Sadducees of the New Testament) or laymen (as were the Pharisees). But the thing that set them apart was community recognition that they were skilled in the Word of God.

These skilled men, the scribes, served on ecclesiastical courts that ruled on all matters of civil and criminal law in Israel. Shortly after the first century the term "rabbi" was reserved for these scholars whose practical duties involved ruling on all sort of cases brought to them.

It was only natural that questions which arose about divorce and remarriage should also be brought to the scribes. As many early Jewish writings show, rabbis and scribes debated the issue of when a person could validly be divorced, and when a person could not. Deuteronomy 24 simply said a husband must give his wife a written paper proving she was divorced, presumably so she could remarry without any question as to whether or not the earlier marriage had been dissolved. While the husband still had to write the bill, ecclesiastical courts of scribes became increasingly involved in divorce cases.

With this context for the question of the Pharisees understood, we can go on to look at Matthew 19 itself.

Some Pharisees came to him to test him. They asked, "Is it lawful for a man to divorce his wife for any and every reason?"

"Haven't you read," he replied, "that at the beginning the Creator 'made them male and female,' and said, 'For this reason a man will leave his father and mother and be united to his wife, and the two will become one flesh'? So they are no longer two, but one. Therefore what God has joined together, let man not separate."

"Why then," they asked, "did Moses command that a man give his wife a certificate of divorce and send her away?"

Jesus replied, "Moses permitted you to divorce your wives because your hearts were hard. But it was not this way from the beginning. I tell you that anyone who divorces his wife, except for marital unfaithfulness, and marries another woman commits adultery."

The disciples said to him, "If this is the situation between a husband and wife, it is better not to marry."

Jesus replied, "Not everyone can accept this teaching, but only those to whom it has been given. For some are eunuchs because they were born that way; others were made that way by men; and others have renounced marriage because of the kingdom of heaven. The one who can accept this should accept it."

Truth. This passage, like Matthew 5, is more concerned with the issue of law than the question of divorce. However, it adds directly to our understanding of why God permitted human beings to divorce in the first place and, by implication, why he permits divorce today.

First, note that God's ideal is a permanent, lifelong relationship. Even "lawful" divorce is a violation of God's ideal will, and thus in essence is sin. In the same way remarriage violates God's ideal and, technically, involves adultery. When Jesus stated this position, the Pharisees were stunned. How then did Jesus explain the fact that Old Testament law makes provision for divorce, and expects remarriage to follow (Deut. 24:1–3)?

Second, note Jesus' answer. God permitted divorce "for the hardness of your hearts." That is, God made provision in his law for the impact of sin on human nature. In going back to the Creation account, Jesus makes reference to Genesis 3 and the entry of sin into our world. Marriage was instituted prior to the entry of sin, and a permanent union remains God's ideal for humankind. But when sin entered with the first couple's disobedience, our experience of the ideal was shattered. What became real was the fact that human hearts are hard. Sin distorted man's relationship with God, but also with other human beings. Out of sinful human hearts selfishness, anger, and hatred were born, along with crime and oppression. Cain killed his brother Abel. And marriage too was affected. In all too many marriages the ideal of oneness and harmony has been twisted into something ugly, painful, and sick.

It is this "hardness of heart," Jesus said, that led God to make provision in his law for divorce, even though divorce is a violation of the ideal, and thus sin. And the need of so many for a loving, caring marriage led God to permit remarriage. God has only permitted divorce because he knows that some marriages are so destructive that they must be ended. And certainly the law that permitted divorce in the Old Testament was always understood to imply the legitimacy of remarriage.

One final note before going on to trace the thought of the extended passage in which this incident is described. Jesus said, "What God has joined together, let man not separate." Isn't this a flat and utterly clear prohibition of divorce? Not at all. First, "what God has joined together" does not mean a specific marriage. The text is not saying that God directed John and Mary to wed, so they cannot divorce. Instead the *institution* of marriage is the issue. God has ordained a relationship which, one entered, men are not competent to break apart. It is here that we need to remember context. In the first century scribes and scribal courts were making pronouncements on when it was valid to divorce, and when it was not. Mere men were making judgments on an institution God had ordained! And *the Old Testament granted no ecclesiastical court that privilege.*

If we go back to Deuteronomy 24 we notice that no court of elders or priests was involved when a divorce took place. It was up to the husband and wife to determine if the marriage was ended. The only legality involved was giving the wife a written bill of divorce and, of course, returning her dowry or any settlement which may have been specified in a marriage contract. Jesus' point is not that a husband and wife are unable to divorce, but that no human ecclesiastical court has any business saying "you can" or "you can't"; "you should" or "you shouldn't"!

What a challenge to us today. We must each bear responsibility for our own choices. Has our marriage reached the point where the hardness of one or both party's heart is so great that to continue together would be destructive? If it has, divorce is an option, although we must not hold on to God's ideal lightly. If we are convinced that divorce we must, we can appeal to no pastor or counselor to validate our decision. The responsibility is ours alone. Yet in that responsibility we experience freedom and grace. We are free from the burden of ecclesiastical courts, and free from the strident demands of those who tell us what we must or cannot do. We are free to seek God's will in our particular case, knowing that divorce is never the ideal, but that in some cases divorce is unquestionably the will of a God who views with such compassion the impact of sin on human lives.

The general argument of the passage, which extends from Matthew 18:1 on through Matthew 20, has already been traced in the chapters of this book. However, a review of the argument may be in order.

The theme of the passage is *greatness*. When his disciples ask about greatness, Jesus shows them a child. Throughout the passage, reference is made to "little ones." In the kingdom, the humility demonstrated by the little child who came when Jesus called is held out as a model. We also are to be responsive to Jesus' words.

Christ then goes on to warn against causing little ones to sin. He gives three illustrations that show us how to live with each other as little ones and protect the quality of responsiveness in each other. First, Jesus says we are sheep who tend to go astray. It's appropriate that straying sheep be sought out and restored with joy rather than recriminations. Second, Jesus says we are brothers in a family who are sure to sin against each other. But when hurts come we are to seek reconciliation through open expression of our hurts and mutual forgiveness. Third, Jesus says that we are servants who have been forgiven a great debt by our King. When we remember how much we have been forgiven, we will find grace to forgive each other.

Greatness, then is found in responsiveness to God, and our responsiveness to God is encouraged and protected by living with each other in reconciling, open, and forgiving ways.

In Matthew 19 Jesus turns to examine three approaches to spiritual greatness espoused by religious men and women of all ages. His first confrontation is with the Pharisees, who see Law and rigorous obedience to Law as the path to greatness. In his exposition on marriage, Jesus demonstrates that Law is a *lower* and not a *higher* standard. God's ideal for marriage is not expressed in the Law, but rather Law is an accommodation of the ideal to the hardness of Israel's sin-warped hearts. Certainly greatness cannnot come through living by a standard which actually lowers God's ideal to accommodate human sinfulness!

The incident with the little children, whom Jesus identifies as possessors of his kingdom, is very significant. Jesus knew that his followers might misunderstand what he was saying about marriage, and try to make it some new and higher law. By identifying the possessors of his kingdom as little children, who under the Jewish system were *not under Law*, Jesus was saying in the clearest possible way that in the kingdom of Christ, God has not and will not relate to the believer through Law. The whole issue of "Is it lawful?" with which the Pharisees were so concerned belonged to another era. Our relationship with God and the principles which govern our lives must be worked out on an entirely different basis than the legal.

The next incident involves a young man who has shown in wonderful humanitarian ways that he has a tender heart for his fellowmen. Jesus, however, confronts him with a strange command. "Go and sell everything you have, . . . and come, follow me" (Matt. 19:21, TLB). The young man, who is wealthy, is stunned. Finally, in sorrow, he turns away from Jesus and returns to his philanthropies. Is Jesus giving a general command that all who have wealth should give it away and follow him in poverty? Not at all. This young man had based his hope of spiritual achievement on living by the second half of the decalog, the commandments governing relationships with other men. Jesus' command to him was a word from his God, the God whom the first commandment insists men love and worship and obey with total commitment. When forced to choose between obedience to God and his wealth, the young man chose wealth. Jesus' command brought the value conflict into the open and revealed to us if not to the young man that *God was not first in his life*. He had broken the first commandment! Philanthropy is good. But it is not a substitute for responsiveness to God.

The third incident, found in Matthew 20:1–16, involves the story of a landowner who hired others to work in his fields. It tells how he contracted with some for a fair day's wage. Through the day, he kept adding workmen, promising only to be fair with them. When the day's work was over, he paid them all. He generously paid the ones who had begun work in the afternoon as much as those who had begun in the morning. Those who worked the full day were angry. But the landowner was firm. He was free to do as he chose with his possessions. And he chose to deal with his workers on the basis of generosity. This story is for those who seek greatness through service. It is for those who mistake frantic activity for service to the Master and who take pride in comparing themselves with those who are not as faithful workers. God will be fair with such people. But true greatness is found in the lifestyle of reconciliation, openness, and forgiveness which help us be responsive to God.

Matthew 20 moves toward a close as two disciples have their mother ask Jesus for important posts in his coming kingdom. This stimulates the final teaching on greatness, in which Jesus contrasts the secular approach, which sees greatness in rule and authority, with the spiritual approach, which sees greatness in servanthood. To give ourselves for others is the mark of spiritual maturity and leadership.

In the final incident, in which Jesus responds to the cry of the blind men, we see greatness personified in our Lord. Setting aside his own deep anguish and need, Jesus asks them simply, "What do you want me to do for you?"

A heart that is tender to the needs of God's little ones is the greatest heart of all.

By seeing the teaching on marriage in this total context, we immediately avoid the common error of those who come to this passage for support of a legalistic approach to divorce and remarriage. Jesus' whole aim in his discussion with the Pharisees, who relied on Law, was to point out the inadequacy of their "Is it lawful?" approach to life. Once again, there is no support at all in this passage for a contemporary legalism that would interpret Jesus as establishing a new law on marriage and divorce.

Grace. It is very helpful to us here to bring a grace perspective into our thinking on this passage, for this passage is one of the most significant in helping us understand how grace operated in Old Testament times.

In Galatians Paul argues that Israel's relationship with God was always based on grace and promise. The Abrahamic Covenant was made some 400 years before Law was given! Whatever Law did, it could not invalidate the promise, or replace promise as a foundation for God/man relationships (Gal. 3:17). Under and through it all there must be grace.

Under Law there was consistent failure . . . but there was also provision. Immediately after the institution of Law in the sequence of Old Testament history we see God giving instructions for the construction of the Tabernacle and the sacrificial system. Men would sin, but the Law made provision for a covering sacrifice for sin until the ultimate` offering might be made by Christ (Rom. 3:24–26). Thus grace, and faith expressed in the bringing of the sacrifice, operated under Law as well as in our New Covenant age.

But there were many who misunderstood the function of Law. Paul says in Romans that Law was intended to speak so clearly to man's failure that "every mouth may be stopped, and the whole world may be held accountable to God. For no human being will be justified in his sight by works of the law, since through the law comes knowledge of sin" (3:19–20, RSV). This function of Law was missed by those like the Pharisees who attempted to use Law for self-justification, and who perceived Law as the *highest possible moral standard.* But this is just the point that Jesus makes in Matthew 19 and that he has also made in Matthew 5! *Law is not the highest possible moral standard! Law is in fact a reduced standard!* God's ideal is for a humanity which so bears his likeness that anger and lust are eradicated. Law sets up standards that deal with the *results* of those inner passions—murder and adultery. God's ideal is for a humanity in which marriage is a perfect oneness state. Law, in recognition of the impact of sin on human relationships, actually permits divorce and remarriage! God in Law showed himself willing to accommodate his ideals to the reality of our tragic human condition. And *this* is *grace.*

Thus grace infused the whole of the old economy as well as our present age. God showed himself willing then, as he is now, to meet with a sin-cursed humanity, to bring us his love and redemption, and to continue to deal gently with us in our awful tension between an ideal we so yearn for and a reality with which we must live. It was the grace of God, expressed in the marriage law and every other law, which should have impressed the religious of Israel. But instead they missed the grace, distorted Law, and went about establishing their own righteousness rather than permitting God to deal with their sin.

Matthew 19 is a stunning revelation of the grace of God. It tells us, in the most powerful terms, that God really does understand the anguish that marks the breakup of a marriage, and that he cares. It reminds us that God is the one who permitted divorce even though it falls so tragically short of his own ideal for us. And it releases from the jurisdiction of all who, like the scribes and Pharisees of Jesus' day, claim the right to sit as an ecclesiastical court and judge our sufferings.

Matthew 19 reminds us that if we are to go on with life we must confess our sins and accept the forgiveness God so richly pours out on sinners. Finally, Matthew 19 gives us confidence. If we grow in a relationship with God which is rooted not in law but in grace, we will become the kind of persons who can reach for the ideal again—and succeed.

12

Mark 10:2–12

Some Pharisees came and tested him by asking, "Is it lawful for a man to divorce his wife?"

"What did Moses command you?" he replied.

They said, "Moses permitted a man to write a certificate of divorce and send her away."

"It was because your hearts were hard that Moses wrote you this law," Jesus replied. "But at the beginning of creation God 'made them male and female.' 'For this reason a man will leave his father and mother and be united to his wife, and the two will become one flesh.' So they are no longer two, but one. Therefore what God has joined together, let man not separate."

When they were in the house again, the disciples asked Jesus about this. He answered, "Anyone who divorces his wife and marries another woman commits adultery against her. And if she divorces her husband and marries another man, she commits adultery."

Context. The context is described at the beginning of chapters 10 and 11.

Truth. In this passage Jesus again goes back to the original creation and expresses the ideal. Once again he does not respond to the initiating question of the Pharisees, which deals with "lawfulness." In this passage no "exception clause" is stated, and it would appear that remarriage, no matter what the cause of the divorce, involves adultery.

At the same time, it is interesting to note that only the one *initiating the divorce* and subsequently remarrying is charged by Christ as committing adultery in this passage. In fact, only in the Matthew 5 passage is there an indication in any Gospel statement that the "innocent party" is also involved in adultery in the establishment of a new union.

The main point here, however, seems to be that Jesus again refuses to deal with the Pharisees on the basis they choose of "lawfulness," and goes back to God's ideal for mankind as the basis for interpreting divorce and remarriage. But again in his explanation of the "hardness of heart" principle, Jesus shows that Law is a demonstration of God's willingness to accommodate himself to human frailty. On the basis of the ideal, which neither Israel as a whole nor the Pharisee alone could achieve, divorce could not be considered. In view of the hardness of heart of human beings, Law permitted divorce and remarriage as a legitimate act.

Argument. The sequence in Mark closely parallels, though it does not duplicate, the sequence of events in Matthew's Gospel. Here too the question of greatness (Mark 9:33–37) precedes Jesus' meeting with the Pharisees, and the incident in which Jesus welcomes the little children and identifies the kingdom of God as "belonging to such as these" immediately follows (10:13–16). Again the sequence of events warns us against erecting into a new law the "no divorce" concept which is implicit in Jesus' ideal and made explicit in his interpretation of its implications.

A chart comparing significant elements in the three extended Gospel passages on divorce and remarriage may be helpful, and is included on the following page.

"What God has joined together, let man not separate."

This formula appears here in Mark, and is also stated in Matthew 19:6. It has been taken by many as conclusive proof that divorce itself is illegitimate.

Such an interpretation of the phrase is not allowable, however, in view of the fact already pointed out in this study: Law, given by God, explicitly recognized the legitimacy of both divorce and remarriage.

How then are we to understand this expression? By returning to an examination of the context. In both Mark and Matthew 19 (but not in Matthew 5 or Luke 16) Jesus' comments on divorce are in response to specific "tests" posed by the Pharisees. The expression "what God has joined let man not separate" is in direct response to the spirit and the letter of their questioning.

The debate in Israel, as I've pointed out earlier, focused not on whether divorce was to be permitted but on the question of *acceptable grounds* for divorce. The issue was simply this: "On what grounds shall we *permit* a divorce to take place?" In raising this kind of question the Pharisees and other religious leaders were arrogating the role of judge, and taking it upon themselves to determine for others when a marriage could be dissolved. In keeping with their pride and arrogance, these men claimed for themselves the right to tell a couple when the marriage covenant was broken and when it was not.

But God has not made men judges over other men! James says, "He that speaks evil against a brother or judges his brother, speaks evil against the law and

	MATTHEW 5	MATTHEW 19	MARK 10
Occasion	Christ "fulfills" the law in response to charge that he is Law's enemy	Pharisees ask about "lawfulness" of divorce for "any cause"	Pharisees ask about "lawfulness" of divorce
Christ's argument	Law is an inadequate expression of God's ideal for man	Law is a lower rather than higher standard	Law is a lower rather than higher standard
Ideal	Not stated	Creation's intended "oneness"	Creation's intended "oneness"
Judgment of divorce	Wrong	Wrong, but permitted because of "hardness of heart"	Wrong, but permitted because of "hardness of heart"
Expected outcome of divorce	Remarriage	Remarriage	Remarriage
Adultery involved	For both parties when either remarries	For the "one divorcing" upon remarriage	For the "one divorcing" upon remarriage
Exception	Divorce for πορνεια (*porneia*)	Divorce for πορνεια (*porneia*)	None stated

judges the law. But if you judge the law, you are not a doer of the law but a judge. There is one lawgiver and judge, he who is able to save and to destroy. But who are you that you judge your neighbor?" (4:11–12, RSV). The intimacy . . . and the agony . . . of the marriage relationship are not open to the judgment of others.

This is totally consistent with the Old Testament divorce procedure. Those whose marriage covenants had been shattered by hardness of heart and the unwillingness of one or both to maintain the relationship went to no court for judgment. No one said "you can" or "you cannot." Instead the course to be followed was determined by the two alone, and the "bill of divorcement," a written release from the relationship, was given signed by the husband to the wife.

But now the Pharisees claimed the right to judge! And they asked Jesus to state the principles upon which *they* would determine *for others* when a divorce could be permitted! Jesus' answer was firm and clear. "What God has joined together, let man not separate." Let no man claim the right to judge and say for others when hardness of heart has already destroyed a relationship which God created, but which man, through loving forgiveness, must seek his grace to restore.

Grace. The question raised, and the answer given, focus on the legal issue. The grace is seen first in Christ's rejection of the right of ecclesiastical courts to judge. Surprisingly, the grace is also seen in Jesus' blunt statement that the remarriage of a person who divorces involves adultery. Where is the grace? In the fact that "Moses wrote you this law!" God demonstrated his grace by permitting a hurting man or woman the option of divorce. For the Christian, divorce will be a last resort, an option taken only when hardness of heart makes the relationship unendurable. God's grace is displayed in that he gives us permission to leave, and permission to try again. The sin of divorce and remarriage is less in God's eye than bondage in a relationship which sin has corrupted and destroyed. Any sin involved in remarriage is less in God's sight than the healing the new relationship can bring. How gracious God is to forgive, and to let us try again.

13

Luke 16:18

"Anyone who divorces his wife and marries another woman commits adultery, and the man who marries a divorced woman commits adultery."

Truth. The realities stated here, and in Matthew 5, deal simply with the impact of remarriage. In this brief statement no expression of the ideal is concluded, although in view of the other Gospel passages the ideal is clearly the basis from which the pronouncement is made.

Argument. This brief statement is placed in an extended discourse without a clear connection to the argument. It seems to be almost a "shot" at the Pharisees, and may be based on the fact that Jesus has stated his argument that Law is a lower standard in previous confrontation, and thus the whole argument is well known to the religious leaders. Not only would it be well known and much discussed, but it would be an argument for which they would have no answer. Thus a mere reference to it might be enough to silence these vocal critics.

The immediate context does show that the statement is directed to the Pharisees:

> The Pharisees, who were lovers of money, heard all this, and they scoffed at him. But he said to them, "You are those who justify yourselves before men, but God knows your hearts; for what is exalted among men is an abomination in the sight of God. The law and the prophets were until John; since then the good news of the kingdom of God is preached, and every one enters it violently. But it is easier for heaven and earth to pass away, than for one dot of the law to become void.— Luke 16:14–17, RSV

It is at this point that Jesus makes his statement about divorce and remarriage.

14

1 Corinthians 7

There are two passages in the Epistles that touch on divorce and remarriage. The first, in Romans 7, uses the "law regarding marriage" in an illustrative way to point out that when one person in a union dies, the other is free from the law of marriage and can remarry without stigma. In the same way, our union with Jesus Christ in his death means that through him we "died" to the Law as a principle of relationship. Our union with Jesus in his resurrection means that our new life with God is based on totally different principles than our old life under Law. We are now related to God and seek responsiveness to God through the Spirit and "not under the old written code" (Rom. 7:6, RSV; see vv. 1–6).

This illustrative use of marriage in a theological argument is not relevant to our exploration of divorce and remarriage. Paul has selected only one point at which to make his comparison. He is not teaching about marriage, but using "the law of marriage" and the freedom of a surviving partner from that law to show the basis on which a Christian's freedom from Law itself can be claimed.

There is, however, an extended New Testament passage that does deal *directly* with the issue of remarriage. This passage in 1 Corinthians 7, as with Matthew 19, is a passage that we must explore carefully. Let's approach it a section at a time.

Context. In 1 Corinthians 7 Paul is writing to a predominantly gentile church in the city of Corinth. The situation in Corinth was very different from that in Judea, where the Gospels are set. The Christian message had been accepted by many in the pagan city, but the implications of the new faith were not fully understood. One area of confusion had to do with sex, and with marriage. This was particularly true in Corinth, which was widely known for sexual looseness. In fact a common phrase, "to Corinthianize," meant immersing oneself in sexual practices which even pagans viewed as scandalous!

Paul had spent months (some say years) in Corinth. And, among the other topics on which he taught, he covered sex and marital relationships. But as always, many of his teachings had been taken out of context, and the confusion caused great concern to Corinthian believers. Among the misunderstandings was the statement, "it is good not to touch a woman," which was variously interpreted as a prohibition against marriage and a demand for a "spiritual marriage" in which sex was set aside. Paul's teachings on yoking with unbelievers led some believing spouses to consider, or actually obtain, divorces. Paul's strong teaching against divorce, based on Jesus' statement of the ideal and his application ("What God has joined, let man not separate") caused much concern to those who had been divorced by pagan spouses.

Remarriage

All of these very practical and very painful issues were shared with the Apostle and, in his first letter back to the Corinthians, he includes a section designed to correct their misunderstandings.

We can see each of these problems emerge as we trace the thought of the Apostle through this chapter of Corinthians. In interpreting this chapter, it is important to do so against the background of the problems just sketched.

Truth. Because this passage is so long, the best way to trace its argument and understand what Paul teaches is to comment on it in sections, as the argument develops.

> Now for the matters you wrote about: It is good for a man not to marry [the RSV translates this, "not to touch a woman"]. But since there is so much immorality, each man should have his own wife, and each woman her own husband. The husband should fulfill his marital duty to his wife, and likewise the wife to her husband. The wife's body does not belong to her alone but also to her husband. In the same way, the husband's body does not belong to him alone but also to his wife. Do not deprive each other except by mutual consent and for a time, so that you may devote yourselves to prayer. Then come together again so that Satan will not tempt you because of your lack of self-control. I say this as a concession, not as a command. I wish that all men were as I am. But each man has his own gift from God; one has this gift, another has that.—1 Corinthians 7:1–7

Comment. This passage is straightforward and clear. Paul never intended to prohibit marriage, nor to command it. He certainly never intended to teach a sexless marriage. In fact, he specifically directs that withdrawal from sexual relations is to be only by mutual consent, for a limited time, and for a specific purpose. Of interest may be the fact that Paul treats the man and woman in the union as having *equal* sexual rights, as well as equal responsibilities. There is no hint here of the "female inferiority" view that so many mistakenly accuse the Apostle of holding.

> To the unmarried and the widows I say that it is well for them to remain single as I do. But if they cannot exercise self-control, they should marry. For it is better to marry than to be aflame with passion.—1 Corinthians 7:8–9, RSV

Comment. Paul has identified sexual need as valid. These needs should be considered in deciding whether to marry. Later Paul will give reasons why he believes the single state is better. Now, building on his awareness that some have one gift, others another (7:7), Paul encourages those with strong sexual drives to consider marriage as best for them.

Paul holds out marriage here as an option to the "unmarried and the widows." Immediately we plunge into the basic issue. Who does Paul think of as "unmarried"? Is it virgins only, who have never been married, or does he include at least some of those who have been divorced?

Terminology. The word translated "unmarried" is ἀγαμοισ *(agamois)*. The word is a compound, made simply from the Greek word for "marry" and the negative prefix α. Etymologically there is no way to tell whether "unmarried" includes the divorced. However, this same word is used by Paul in 1 Corinthians 7:11 of a divorced woman. While we cannot conclude from this usage that Paul includes the divorced in verse 8 when he advises marriage for those with dominating sexual needs, we certainly *can* conclude that neither the meaning of the word, nor Paul's use of it, requires that we view "unmarried" here as virgins only.

It is even possible to argue that Paul does include the divorced in his advice to remarry under this sexual need condition.

> To the married I give this command (not I, but the Lord): A wife must not separate from her husband. But if she does, she must remain unmarried or else be reconciled to her husband. And a husband must not divorce his wife.—1 Corinthians 7:10–11

Comment. It's clear that, as from the Beginning, the ideal for marriage must set our standards. Thus it follows that it is God's will that a marriage involve a permanent, lifelong relationship. Paul quotes Jesus' restatement of that ideal and his application: "what God has joined let no man put asunder." Christians, above all others, with the resource of God's Spirit to lift us above the limitations placed on humanity by sin, must uphold the ideal and commit ourselves to achieve it.

Certainly those who thought they were pleasing God by divorcing misunderstood Paul's teaching. Jesus' own words confirmed marriage as a God-ordained state. Divorce is not what God wants for his people. Paul states this forcefully. And no wonder! One of the characteristic ideas that false teachers introduced into the Church is expressed in 1 Timothy 4:3: they "forbid marriage and enjoin abstinence from foods which God created to be received with thanksgiving by those who believe and know the truth" (RSV). No, the Lord's will is clear: marriage unions are not to be broken or put aside by men—even for "spiritual" reasons. Jesus expects us to find grace within the relationship, not by denying its validity.

Paul then is totally confident as he counters the "divorce for spirituality" concept some had promoted at Corinth. Wives are not to separate. Husbands are not to divorce.

Terminology. One question that is immediately raised in this context is whether or not there is a difference between "separate" and "divorce" in these verses.

The word for "separate" is χωρισθῆναι *(choristhe-nai)*. In the active it means to "divide, or separate" something. In the passive it means "separate (oneself)" or "be separated." It is used in the Greek language of divorce. In fact, it is used often and specifically of the breaking of marriage contracts.

The word for "divorce" is ἀφιέναι *(aphienai)*, literally "to send away" or "cancel." It too is used in a legal sense of divorce.

Thus the original language makes it clear that Paul is not talking about two different actions which might be taken to adjust a marriage relationship. Our contemporary "legal separation" in contrast to a "decree of divorce" is not implied. Paul is speaking very clearly in both cases of divorce.

Comment. What is most striking in this brief paragraph is the sentence nestled between the two statements prohibiting divorce. "But if she does, she must remain unmarried or else be reconciled to her husband."

Paul has just stated, in a form which seems to admit no possible exceptions, a "must" for believers. "Do not divorce" is certainly God's will. It is certainly the ideal toward which each of us will strive. But it is clear that Paul *expects* that some will not experience the ideal and *will* divorce.

So Paul adds something new in the Bible's discussion of this area. In each of the Gospel accounts, remarriage is assumed to follow divorce. We see this in the juxtaposition of "divorces" and "marries" in each of the accounts. For instance, Mark 10:12 says, "if she di-

vorces her husband and marries another man. . . ."
In the flow of events, it would seem that remarriage
is the expected outcome of divorce. But at just this
point Paul adds a new guideline. This guideline, like
the "no divorce" statement, is one that on its surface
seems exceptionless: "she must remain unmarried or
else be reconciled to her husband."

The difficulty in treating this statement as exceptionless is that statements which appear to be in exceptionless form have biblical exceptions added! For
instance, Mark 10:11–12 states the following exceptionless form that makes it sound like an absolute.
"Anyone who divorces his wife and marries another
woman commits adultery against her. And if she divorces her husband and marries another man, she commits adultery." Yet Jesus himself in Matthew is quoted
as adding the exception, "except for *porneia.*"

Paul's statement in our Corinthians passage, "a wife
must not separate from her husband," also sounds like
an absolute. We would feel a necessity to treat it as
an absolute . . . if Paul did not himself show that
he does not *expect* everyone, in every case, to remain
married by adding, "But if she does, she must remain
unmarried or else be reconciled."

The problem we are faced with, then, is a simple
one. How can we tell when a teaching given in exceptionless form is actually intended to be taken as an
absolute? The warning we need to take seriously is
found in the fact that not all statements in exceptionless form are exceptionless. Therefore we cannot argue
an absolute prohibition on the form alone! Thus the
fact that the teaching "if she does, she must remain
unmarried or else be reconciled to her husband" *seems*
to permit no other option *does not necessarily mean
that there is no other option.*

It is clear, of course, that the "remain unmarried"
directive is in general the best or most desirable course.

At the least we would take it as a guiding principle. But at this point in Paul's argument we cannot tell whether there is in fact no alternative to this pathway, or, if other options do exist, how to know when it is valid to choose them.

> To the rest I say, not the Lord, that if any brother has a wife who is an unbeliever, and she consents to live with him, he should not divorce her. If any woman has a husband who is an unbeliever, and he consents to live with her, she should not divorce him. For the unbelieving husband is consecrated through his wife, and the unbelieving wife is consecrated through her husband. Otherwise, your children would be unclean, but as it is they are holy.—1 Corinthians 7:12–14, RSV

Comment. This is a fascinating passage, with much that might be examined. But for the sake of brevity we need to limit ourselves to the contribution made to the present subject. That contribution is a simple one. Christians are not to initiate divorces even when the spouse is not a Christian. If the unbeliever is willing to live with the believer, then the teaching of Paul not to "be mismated with unbelievers" (2 Cor. 6:14, RSV) does not apply. Elsewhere Paul explains: "Everyone should remain in the state in which he was called" (1 Cor. 7:20, RSV).

> But if the unbeliever leaves, let him do so. A believing man or woman is not bound in such circumstances; God has called us to live in peace. How do you know, wife, whether you will save your husband? Or, how do you know, husband, whether you will save your wife—1 Corinthians 7:15–16

Comment. Our first observation is that here is comfort for the Christians who were abandoned by their non-

Remarriage

Christian spouses, and who were tormented by the doubt about whether *they* had sinned through the divorce.

Paul clearly suggests with the phrase "let him do so" that the Christian is not to make unusual efforts to save the marriage and need not accept responsibility for the breakup.

However, what is even more significant is that *just a few verses after making an apparently exceptionless statement ("remain unmarried or be reconciled") Paul has himself introduced an exception!* The exception is found in the clause "a believing man or woman is not bound in such circumstances," and is explained in the rest of this short segment.

Terminology. The word for "bound" here is δεδούλωται *(dedoulotai)*, which in this verb form might be paraphrased "to be in a continuing state of bondage." Paul's point is that the bondage to the husband or wife, which is generally conceived of as a "marriage bond," *no longer continues.* The marriage bond is broken, and the divorced believer may consider himself or herself *unmarried.* Andre Bustanoby comments on this passage:

> There is no uniform opinion whether being free from bondage means being free to remarry. A great deal of argument has centered on the word *leaves.* What does it mean—divorce or separation? The Greek word for "leave," *koridzetai,* is the same word used in I Corinthians 7:11 to mean divorce, with the condition of remaining unmarried. Otherwise, as I noted in chapter 4, Paul would not have laid out the conditions in which remarriage is wrong. In verses 10–15, Paul uses the word *leave* to mean divorce with or without condition. In verse 15, he speaks of divorce with no condition attached. The clear meaning of verses 10–11 is that the brother or sister *is* under bondage—no remarriage. In verse 15, the brother or sister is *not* under bondage—remarriage is allowed. Indeed, the

believer who is free of the marriage but not free to remarry would still be under bondage. What's more, if legitimate divorce does dissolve a marriage, remarriage is not prohibited, as in the case of Matthew 19:9 with the sin of *porneia.*

Paul does not elucidate the circumstances of verse 15. He does not say whether it applies only to a person who becomes a Christian after marriage or to a believer who unwisely marries an unbeliever. Paul's teaching applies to the situation as it stands at the moment of divorce—an unbeliever who wants to divorce the believer. It matters not how the believer came to be married to the unbeliever. If the unbeliever wants a divorce, the believer is free of the marriage and free to remarry.*

The important thing here is that divorce, with the option of remarriage, *is* a biblical position! The statement about remaining unmarried or being reconciled is not an exceptionless statement whatever its form, for Paul himself almost immediately adds an exception!

But notice Paul's *reasoning* for granting this exception: "How do you know, wife, whether you will save your husband? Or, how do you know, husband, whether you will save your wife?" It is hypothetically possible that an unbeliever who divorces a believer might at a later time be converted, and the marriage union reestablished. But there is no basis for *expecting* this will happen. The possibility of such reconciliation is not sufficient to require the believer to wait. There is an uncertainty about the future, perhaps even a probability of no such sequence of events. Without the *knowledge* (which we can soften if we will to the *likelihood*) of reconciliation, freedom from the need to remain unmarried is proclaimed!

If Paul had simply stated this exception without spelling out the rationale, we might still be without

* Andre Bustanoby, *But I Don't Want a Divorce* (Grand Rapids, MI: Zondervan Publishing House, 1978), p. 280.

clear guidance. But the statement of Paul's rationale does give us principles on which to operate. The principle is one of probability or likelihood of reconciliation. In general we would counsel, "wait." Keep the door open to reconciliation. But at the same time, in many cases there are no grounds to believe in the *probability* of reconciliation. Then we too can perhaps proclaim freedom.

This is the rationale behind the selection of the particular case histories included in the book. In the case of the husband whose wife has remarried, there is no possibility of reconciliation. Surely the "not bound" principle applies here. In the case of the young woman whose non-Christian husband did depart in fact, although it was she who filed for the divorce, Paul's explicit teaching on Christian/non-Christian marriages clearly applies. She is not bound. In the case where the husband left the family to establish a live-in homosexual relationship with another man, there is again no reasonable probability of reconciliation. And in the case of the husband whose wife's mental illness has led to a divorce in fact, and may lead to a legal divorce as well, there would again seem no reasonable likelihood of reconciliation. In all these cases, following the rationale Paul gives for his exception to the "remain unmarried or be reconciled" statement, we can assume that a "not bound" judgment applies.

Grace. What a clear revelation of God's grace. God meets us at each stage of our dilemma with a word of guidance and support. Try to stay together. If you can't, keep the door open to reconciliation. If that door is closed—and only you can judge when it is shut—you are not under bondage. Through divorce you join the ranks of the unmarried and, although you need not marry again, you can.

But if you do, marry "in the Lord."

This time choose a mate who has the same source of grace you have: a relationship with Jesus Christ, who teaches us a commitment, a forgiveness, and an understanding that can make our remarriage succeed.

Freedom and Grace

At this point we have covered the passages from the Gospels and Epistles which add directly to our understanding of divorce/remarriage for Christians. Summarizing the data from these passages, we can conclude:

1. God's Creation ideal of a permanent oneness relationship is, and has always been, the fullest expression of God's will for mankind.

2. The Old Testament introduced a divorce/remarriage option because of the hardness of man's heart, and because of the ravaging impact of sin on this as on all other human relationships.

3. The divorce/remarriage option was *permitted*, but was not in any sense actively encouraged.

4. Divorce and remarriage, during the Old Testament period as well as prior to and subsequent to that time,

will in some cases involve adultery. In such a case God's forgiveness is available, and the second marriage itself is not a "state of sin," but legitimate. In other cases where the divorce comes through "hardness of heart" and because of falling short rather than willful sin, Jesus' exception principle applies. In this case remarriage is free from even the technical charge of adultery, for marriage contracts broken by the willful action of another leaves the deserted partner "not bound."

5. In the New Testament, the Creation ideal is restated (as it was in Mal. 2) as the goal to which believers should strive. What is more, Matthew 18 carefully describes relational principles on which to build a marriage, even though both partners are affected by sin. This pattern involves a commitment to seek reconciliation, an openness when hurt, and a freely given and received forgiveness.

6. The statements in the New Testament of God's will for permanency in the marriage relationship are not to be viewed by us as either new law or as the statement of an exceptionless absolute. This is seen from the fact that while teachings on marriage and instructions to the unmarried are often given in exceptionless *form*, the Bible itself goes on to specify exceptions. This is also seen in Christ's statement of "except for *porneia*" and in Paul's dual statement of exceptions in 1 Corinthians 7.

7. Granting that the statements on marriage and divorce, though in exceptionless form, are not exceptionless, we can still develop a clear set of guidelines for Christians in troubled marriages. These involve first of all a personal responsiveness to Jesus as he speaks God's ideal and sets forth the will of God in marriage. Given, however, that for some reason it is not possible

(and here the reality of sin in hardening human hearts is the basic reason in some cases that it is *not* possible to save a marriage), the pattern the believer is to follow is this one:

(1) Seek through the Matthew 18 pattern to be reconciled within the relationship. This corresponds to Paul's repeated statement "a husband (or wife) must not divorce" the spouse.

(2) If in spite of every effort a divorce must take place, then the believer is "to remain unmarried or to be reconciled." This principle of an open door to return is an important one, and each Christian who experiences the anguish of separation should prayerfully consider a commitment to remain unmarried until reconciliation can come.

(3) However, the unmarried state is *not* to be seen as the only option. Paul immediately states an exception in the case of unbelievers who divorce their believing spouses. They are "not bound," Paul says (the same term he uses in 1 Cor. 7:39 to speak of the binding quality of marriage). Paul gives as a basis for this judgment the fact that we cannot in some cases reasonably expect reconciliation to occur.

This statement of *likelihood* of reconciliation is extremely significant. It is *not* a license to blithely say, "Good. I don't think *we'll* ever get back together, and therefore I can remarry." It is, however, a grace principle that finds beautiful expression in Paul's word of compassion, "God has called us to live in peace" (7:15).

8. Within the framework provided by these principles, we are justified in concluding that the God who calls us to peace and who showed his willingness to deal graciously with his Old Testament people when sin's hardness destroyed a marriage continues to deal with us in grace. Without denying the ideal, the Church should give compassionate guidance to those troubled

thousands who deeply desire to please God but who find that their gift is the married state (7:7), and who often are in bitter conflict over the legalistic teaching and attitudes of the Christian community.

The terrible tendency to which we are all subject is to legalize grace. Somehow we feel that we have to translate guiding principles in the Word into legalistic structures. I am very aware that those who read this book, even those who are persuaded to the position to which I have come (to my own surprise!), will tend immediately to fall into the legalistic trap. Following are some of the signs of legalizing the concepts I've presented.

* When some ask, "*When* is there no likelihood of reconciliation? When can we permit marriage on this ground?"
* When some say, "Of course, this applies only to the *innocent* party in the broken marriage. The one whose hardness of heart was the cause of the breakup is not free to 'benefit' from his or her sin."
* When some insist, "You must of course keep the door to reconciliation open for a minimum of two years." Or five. Or seven.
* When some ask, "Who *determines* when remarriage is valid? The pastor? The church board, acting as an ecclesiastical court?"
* When some ask, "Does 'divorces his wife' in the Gospels mean the one who takes the legal action, or the one who is really 'at fault'?"

By such questions, even this grace-based teaching will be squeezed into legal form by those who are moved by fear and distrust to set up restrictions and attempt to control others.

In 2 Corinthians, Paul sets us a very different example. In chapters 8 and 9 he is dealing with giving (something else that we legalize with teaching about tithing). There Paul very clearly states the realities on which Christian giving is based, and desires that the people of that city will give generously. Yet in the context of his argument, Paul takes great care to *preserve the freedom of the men and women of Corinth.*

Paul is, as in the case of divorce and remarriage, communicating truth which is an expression of God's will. He felt free in 1 Corinthians 7 to quote Jesus' instructions as a command (though he himself immediately went on to exceptions). But here there is no specific word from Jesus, so Paul abandons that form. What he says, however, shows us clearly that God does not rely on command to control behavior because, as we saw in Matthew 5, God is concerned about the inner man—the heart.

> I say this not as a command, but to prove by the earnestness of others that your love also is genuine. For you know the grace of our Lord Jesus Christ, that though he was rich, yet for your sake he became poor, so that by his poverty you might become rich. . . .
> Each one must do as he has made up his mind, not reluctantly or under compulsion, for God loves a cheerful giver.—2 Corinthians 8:8–9; 9:7, RSV

Paul refuses to utilize any means to *control the behavior* of these believers. The reason is that God, who loves the cheerful giver, is ultimately concerned with heart-response to him!

Only by removing threat and compulsion as methods of control can the Christian leader free the believer for a heart-response to God. And it is *this* which God seeks above all. No wonder Matthew 18 begins with a picture of greatness as childlike humility which responds to the word and call of Jesus!

But can we *trust* Christians to make the right choices

if we do not treat the issue of divorce and remarriage as a matter of law? Isn't it better to set up legalistic barriers to the behaviors we believe are questionable, so our brothers and sisters will be protected from themselves?

In Romans Paul states a basic truth which we can take as our charter to extend freedom to let our brothers and sisters make their own choices within the framework provided by the Word of God. The teaching is in the context of a warning against taking it upon ourselves to serve as judges of our brothers. Listen.

Who are you to pass judgment on the servant of another? It is before his own master that he stands or falls. And he will be upheld, for the Master is able to make him stand. . . .

For to this end Christ died and lived again, that he might be Lord both of the dead and of the living.

Why do you pass judgment on your brother? Or you, why do you despise your brother?—Romans 14:4, 9–10, RSV

The point is clear.

Jesus is Lord.

Jesus is able to lead our brother or sister into that choice which expresses the will of God for him or her. *We have no right to lord it over a fellow Christian, to demand he or she conform to our understanding of Scripture, or to look down on those who have made a different choice than we might!*

What about Church discipline? In some areas the Body is to agree with God and exercise a discipline designed to restore. If remarriage were unquestionably and always wrong, we should consistently exercise discipline in this area. But remarriage is a valid option, a legitimate act. Here there is individual guidance from Scriptures and Spirit, and freedom to select under

Remarriage

God's leading. The question of discipline does not apply.

The conclusion?

We can only heal, and help, our many brothers and sisters who have suffered deeply in their marriages because of hardness of heart by affirming the position indicated by both Scripture and grace. We can only heal and help in the Christian community by affirming remarriage as a *legitimate* option provided by God.

Appendix

Questions and Objections from Readers

Questions, comments, and objections to the view expressed here have been raised by various readers. Many are included here, with my response. Additional comments that you may have can be addressed to Dr. Larry Richards in care of Word Books, Editorial Dept., Waco, Texas, 76796 for possible inclusion in future editions of the book. If you wish a personal answer, please enclose a self-addressed, stamped envelope.

"This book is a clear case of starting with human experience rather than God's Word to develop a distorted theology."

Not at all. It's a case of human experiences driving me to Scripture to restudy what God's Word teaches. In the process I was led, against my earlier impressions, to the conclusion that the theological understanding traditionally accepted is not biblical at all, and does not communicate God's will accurately to the many who need this area of biblical teaching today.

Remarriage

"Isn't what you are doing adding to the already tragic situation in which Christians accept divorce as the easy way out? I fear that people will take this book as justification for getting divorces, when otherwise they might stay together and work through their problems."

It's possible that some will misunderstand what I've said and even misuse it to justify sin. Paul faced the same problem when teaching about grace and foresaw the misinterpretation, "Let's sin then, that grace may abound" (see Rom. 6:1). "God forbid!" that reaction, Paul said. But he continued to proclaim the grace of God.

I have to say the same thing about distorting this view of remarriage. God forbid that any take it as justification for divorce or for their own choice to turn away from Christ's way of greatness and forgiveness which would maintain the marriage (cf. chap. 2). But can we turn away from proclaiming God's grace because some might misuse it?

Actually, this book is written not to people who are *considering* divorce but to those who have gone through that experience and are either considering remarriage, or have remarried. It's written to people who hurt because they have been told that God has no grace available for them in their situation. It was written because I've come to believe that the teaching in this book is a closer approximation of what the Bible teaches than the "no remarriage" position taken in so many of our churches.

"As a minister I will never marry a couple when this involves remarriage for one or both, unless the earlier partner has already remarried someone else."

It's important for you to do what you believe to be right in obedience to your understanding of Scripture. But it's also important to give others the freedom to be responsible to God for their understanding. All

142

of us have to be careful to resist the temptation to make our own understanding the rule for others.

I find when I am in a situation like yours the best thing I can do is to explain my own understanding of Scripture and encourage the individuals to study and pray the passages through for themselves. Then I'll try to keep a nonjudgmental attitude toward them, letting Christ be Lord in their lives and not insisting they obey *me*.

You may not agree with their conclusions and leading, and thus not feel free yourself to participate in the ceremony. In this case you certainly should not. But be careful not to "forbid" the couple from acting on their own convictions, just as you act on yours.

"I wonder about the sharp contrast you draw between ideals and reality. Do we ever set our ideals too low? May we expect from Christians some kind of growth in grace, so as time goes by we set higher ideals for ourselves?"

I'm sorry that point was confusing. Actually, God's ideal is something we all are to strive toward. And, in Christ, the "grace to help" is designed to bring us to an experience of the ideal. The tension comes when sin intrudes and frustrates our efforts. Then we discover the reality of our experience is often so far from the goal God sets and that we affirm.

The key question then is, how do we respond when we fall short? Also, how does God respond when we fall short? It's here that we need, and obtain, mercy at the throne of grace. God enters with forgiveness to heal and to set us again on our journey toward the ideal.

As chapter 9 points out, in marriage we handle the tension by admitting our failures, forgiving, and letting God rebuild the relationship. When one or both individuals in a marriage *refuse* to deal with this tension between their ideals and the reality of their experience, and when some even go so far as to divorce, we then have to deal with the reality of that fact in tension with our ideal.

What some have done is to teach that when a marriage has failed, there is no "second chance." What I have suggested is that the Bible does *not* close the door to remarriage . . . or back away from the ideal of a single, permanent union.

What do we do when, through sin's hardness of heart, grace *in* marriage has been rejected and a divorce has come? We realize that this area of sin, like all other falling short, is dealt with by God by first forgiveness and then enablement to reach out through failure to his redeeming success. And, in some cases where God so leads, there will be a remarriage in which we continue to strive toward God's ideal.

"When you say that Marilyn's tears are also an expression of mankind's hardness of heart, are you saying only that she is the victim of a sinful husband?"

Yes, and no. There are situations in which we suffer innocently because of another person's sinful choices. It's important to recognize this and not load ourselves down with false guilt or try to shoulder the blame for choices that another person freely makes. At the same time, it's important to realize that in marriage, as in all other relationships, we *participate in the situation*. Isaiah cried out to God confessing, "I am a man of unclean lips, and I dwell in the midst of a people of unclean lips" (Isa. 6:5, KJV). So while we are not to blame ourselves for choices another has made, at the same time we are never to claim, "I'm innocent; none of it was my fault."

"I have a different notion of 'law' than the one in this book. Law isn't just a second-rate codification of God's will, in which he accommodates his standards to our weakness, nor is it an unreachable goal. It's a guide for living."

I don't want to suggest that what the Law says is not holy, just, and good. It is. And, because the Law expresses something of God's own character, we *can* be guided by Law in our living. In fact, the New Testament makes it clear that anyone walking with God and empowered by his Spirit will in fact fulfill the Law (Rom. 8:4).

The point I tried to make is this: Law does not *perfectly* or *ultimately* express God's ideal. His ideal is even higher than Law, reaching beyond behavior into the very motives and inner life of the heart.

When the Pharisees acted as if Law were *all*, they put the focus on externals rather than on inner realities. This of course was Jesus' own evaluation of them: they paid attention to details of Law while neglecting the weightier matters of justice and mercy and faith (Matt. 23:23–24). To make a legal approach to Christian experience everything is to fall into the trap of the Pharisees. So we always want to be sure we recognize that God's revelation is a total kind of thing, with goals and standards, yes. And also with justice and mercy as parts of the total picture.

As far as the Old Testament law concerning divorce is concerned, it definitely was an accommodation to our human situation. It served as evidence that God's ideals (in this case, oneness in a permanent relationship) are not of such an austere nature that they rule out the operation of mercy where sin has thwarted our efforts to achieve the ideal.

"I think the 'fear of grace' you describe on page 58 is more subtle than you give it credit for being. It seems to me those who are afraid of grace are not only threatened by declining standards, but also by the loss of justification for their own good behavior and self-denial. This 'elder brother' syndrome might well be part of the reason for much opposition to divorce and remarriage in the church."

Yes.

Remarriage

"On page 51 you dismiss the notion that Eve, having been created later, was inferior to Adam. But doesn't Paul make that very point in 1 Timothy 2:13?"

No. Paul's point is that men and women are *different*. Not that one is superior or inferior.

"Some might rightly be alarmed by your suggestion (p. 70) that the existence of one exception to a moral proscription implies the existence of other exceptions as well."

It does not necessarily imply the existence of other exceptions. It simply demonstrates that the proscription is *not exceptionless*. I think that Paul's argument in 1 Corinthians 7:16 in which he explains why he makes the exception is critical. When he says that a believer separated (divorced) from an unbeliever is not under bondage *because* no likelihood of reconciliation can be argued, we do have grounds to apply the same reasoning to other divorce situations.

"How do we know? How do we know there will never be the kind of healing for Linda that will make a meaningful marriage relationship possible? From exactly the opposite point of view, how did the Lord show Ann (p. 63) that she ought not to remarry?"

We don't *know*. That's always the problem in walking by faith: since we cannot be sure of the outcome of any specific situation, we are thrown back on God for his personal guidance and leading.

It's really impossible to say "how" the Lord shows us his will. We do know that as a living Person, Jesus is able to communicate with us. We know the Holy Spirit is present in our lives. We know the Bible speaks about hearing God's voice and being led by the Spirit. And we each know that we have had experiences in which we made choices because we believed they were God's will for us.

This is the thing that is important for us. Not the *how*. But the reality. God *does* speak to us and guide us. And each of us is to be responsive to the Lord.

"Who helps the individual to decide these issues? You are quite explicit in rejecting the notion that the church or its officials ought to stand in judgment in such situations. Yet isn't there a sense in which our own capacity for accurate perception is seriously dimmed by sin? Isn't there a danger that we might be inclined to give ourselves the benefit of the doubt? We must be willing to submit our ethical judgments to the advice of others before availing ourselves of the permission to remarry which this book describes."

These are good points. I believe that all of us need to be in submission to three valid lines of spiritual authority. The first is Scripture, the second is the traditional understanding of Scripture's teachings (as expressed, for example, in the creedal confessions of the Church), and the third is the voice of brothers and sisters with whom we live in fellowship.

It's important, however, to see what each of these lines of spiritual authority contributes in our decisional process. Scripture contributes an objective check on our perceptions—God's revelation of reality always stands above and in judgment of my ideas, desires, motives, and goals. I search the Scriptures to understand the mind and will of God *in general,* and affirm that I will not be led by God into actions which are contrary to God's revealed will (for instance, the Spirit will never lead me to commit adultery).

The voice of the Church through the ages aids me in evaluating my own understanding of Scripture's message. If my interpretation is contrary to the understanding of the Church historically, then I am probably wrong. Note here, however, that the voice of the Church historically focuses on common understanding of doctrinal core truths.

Finally, the Christian community of which I am a part is also vital. But the contribution here is not so much one of interpreting the Scriptures or standing in judgment over my choices as it is of guarding my heart and motives so that I truly seek God's will and not my own. Personally, I find it important to submit to significant brothers in my own life, not so that they make my decisions for me, but so that they test me at every point to guard my motives and my desire to please God. Since Jesus died and rose again to be Lord of every one of us (Rom. 14:9), I must submit to him as Lord of my life and be obedient to him. He is Lord—not my fellow Christians. But my fellow Christians are important to guard my decision-making process and to be sure that my heart is right. They may disagree with my decision, but if they are convinced that I am honestly seeking to do God's will as I understand it, they will not stand in judgment over me or the decision I am led to.

"I guess I am a little fearful that what you write will be interpreted too readily by someone who has not yet taken the step of divorce as an encouragement to give up on the first marriage with the hope of doing better the next time."

Again, I hope not.

To the married, the message of Scripture and this book is, follow God's prescription for building your relationship and healing it (chap. 2).

To the divorced and already remarried, the message of Scripture and this book is, recognize the roots of the broken relationship as sin, and yet realize that God deals even with this in grace and forgiveness. And that his gift of forgiveness includes the possibility of remarriage.

To the divorced but not yet remarried, the message of Scripture and this book is, you *may* remarry. But be sure that God is actively leading you into such a relationship. Commit yourself to his good will, whatever it may involve: a life of singleness or a life of marriage.